P9-DCJ-929

Successful enquiry answering every time

Successful enquiry answering every time

The sixth edition of Tim Buckley Owen's classic *Success at the Enquiry Desk*

Fully revised and updated

Tim Buckley Owen

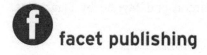

facet publishing

© Tim Buckley Owen 1996, 1997, 1998, 2000, 2003, 2006, 2012

Published by Facet Publishing
7 Ridgmount Street, London WC1E 7AE
www.facetpublishing.co.uk

Facet Publishing is wholly owned by CILIP: the Chartered Institute of Library
and Information Professionals.

Tim Buckley Owen has asserted his right under the Copyright, Designs and
Patents Act 1988 to be identified as author of this work.

Except as otherwise permitted under the Copyright, Designs and Patents Act
1988 this publication may only be reproduced, stored or transmitted in any
form or by any means, with the prior permission of the publisher, or, in the
case of reprographic reproduction, in accordance with the terms of a licence
issued by The Copyright Licensing Agency. Enquiries concerning
reproduction outside those terms should be sent to Facet Publishing, 7
Ridgmount Street, London WC1E 7AE.

British Library Cataloguing in Publication Data
A catalogue record for this book is available from the British Library.

ISBN 978-1-85604-811-8

First published 2012

Mixed Sources
Product group from well-managed
forests and other controlled sources
www.fsc.org Cert no. SA-COC-156
© 1996 Forest Stewardship Council

FSC

Text printed on FSC accredited material.

Typeset from author's files in 11/14 pt Minion and Myriad by Flagholme
Publishing Services.
Printed and made in Great Britain by MPG Books Group, UK.

Dedication

To my wife Barbara for her constant support and encouragement now and always. Despite a busy schedule of her own, she read every word of the book in draft and offered her invaluable comments. I frequently resisted her advice, but almost always ended up taking it.

Contents

Introduction

How this book can help you

In December 1995, I rented a small cottage on the Isle of Wight and hired a large and clunky computer from a local firm (for rather more than the cost of renting the cottage) to draft the first edition of this book. Little did I imagine that, sixteen years later, people would still be finding it a useful guide to the complexity and richness of enquiry answering. When I was writing that first edition, people were already predicting that the embryonic world wide web would eventually sound the death knell of flesh and blood enquiry services. As the continuing demand for revised versions of the book demonstrates, how spectacularly wrong they've been proved.

With almost universal access to the web in the developed world and its growing availability in developing nations, especially through mobile technology, people's ability to satisfy their curiosity has been enormously increased and their awareness of information and the tools that make it available has grown hugely. Now we have the arrival of mobile social media, giving everybody the opportunity to contribute to the body of knowledge wherever they are. So the information skill stakes have been raised in ways that were simply unimaginable back then.

This means that it's up to us, as professional enquiry answerers, to ensure that we can always add value to what information users can do for themselves. How? By anticipating problems before they happen. By not simply knowing where to look for the answer but knowing the best place to look – even before we know where that is. By searching smarter – not just putting a few words into a search engine and hoping for the best. By being able to guarantee that the enquirer can trust the information they find. And by recommending the best version of the answer when there are several possibilities available.

So who is this book for? Basically, it's for anyone whose job is to offer information, advice and guidance using third-party sources to help them. So it's definitely for library staff, whether they work in a reference and information service or not. And it's for knowledge and information managers, who may be operating out of their own information unit or embedded within a specialist team. It can also help anyone who works in a contact centre, perhaps dealing with information enquiries, or processing transactions or trouble-shooting technical issues. And it doesn't matter whether your job is actually finding answers for people (working for a company, not-for-profit organization or public body), or helping others find the answers for themselves (as in a public or college library). This book is for you.

Chapter 1 deals with the most fundamental aspect of enquiry answering: finding out what the enquirer really wants. It doesn't matter whether your job is to find the answer for them, or help them with advice and guidance on the strategies they could employ and the sources they might use – get this bit wrong and everything else goes wrong too. Chapter 2 looks at broadly the same thing – but when the enquirer is somewhere else and you have only a voice on the phone or characters on a screen to go by. We normally rely so heavily on non-verbal communication that, when we can't see or hear the enquirer, even more can go wrong – so this chapter tries to help you make sure that it doesn't.

Chapter 3 is all about dealing with the panic that can grip you when the enquirer has made clear what they want and is waiting for you to come up with a solution. Again, it doesn't matter whether you're advising a student or member of the public or embarking on a piece of desk research for a client – it's your job to think your way through the problem clearly. And in Chapter 4, we look at how smarter searching can help produce results that the enquirer simply wouldn't have thought of for themselves – how you can either delight a research client or provide valuable learning support to a student or library visitor.

In Chapter 5, we think about what to do when things start going wrong – when the answer just isn't showing up anywhere and time's running out. You could be coming up to a deadline imposed by your boss or helping a hapless student who just hasn't given themselves enough time to do their assignment; either way, they're looking to you to come up with a plan B. By contrast, Chapter 6 is about success, and how you can add value to your answer – turning it into a readable report for your client, showing a member of the public or a student how they can evaluate what they've found instead of just taking it on trust. This chapter also demonstrates how you can use the results of completed enquiries to measure your performance and provide an even better service.

Chapter 7 takes a look into the future – your next job or role and a new enquiry service to set up or a run-down one to revive. It's all about studying your users' needs – whether they are your colleagues, outside clients, a student community or simply anyone who comes in or phones up – and making sure you have the tools to satisfy them. And finally, Chapter 8 suggests what some of those tools might be: search engines (there's more than one!); enquiry management systems (to help you keep track of your workload); and Starter Sources (multipurpose information resources that can help you begin on a great many of the kinds of enquiries you're likely to encounter).

So it really doesn't matter where you work or who your clientele is, whether you're doing the work yourself or helping others to do it – this book should contain masses of ideas for you. They're not all my ideas of course. Many of them have come from the hundreds of people who've attended my training courses over the years and given fellow participants the benefit of their own experience. When their ideas have struck me as being particularly useful, I have stolen them shamelessly and included them here. So thanks very much to all of them – and to you, for continuing to find this little book useful. I hope you find it an enjoyable read too.

Tim Buckley Owen

Eight ideas for successful enquiry answering

1 Never take an enquiry at face value, always ask a question back – because you never know where it may lead.
2 With remote enquiries you are deprived of most of the clues that we take for granted when dealing with people face to face – so make sure you really do understand what they want.
3 Start by imagining what the final answer will look like – that will help you focus on the best sources and delivery media for the job.
4 Your enquirer has access to the same search engines as you do – your job is to add value by using professionally edited sources and smarter searching.
5 If you can't find the answer, ask yourself who really needs to know this – that should give you ideas for who to ask for help.
6 Make sure you always add value when presenting your answer – that will demonstrate your professionalism.
7 Make sure your service always reflects your enquirers' needs – not the resources you happen to have.
8 Just a few key sources can get you started on a lot of enquiries.

CHAPTER 1

What do you really want?

How to make sure you really understand the question

In this chapter you'll find out how to:

- **avoid misunderstandings**
- **ask the right questions**
- **agree the task**
- **find out how long you've got to do it.**

Picture the scene. You're in the kitchen getting ready for a dinner party and you think your partner has just said: 'Have you got the time?' So you could reply: 'It's ten to eight and the guests are going to be here any moment so let's get on with it.' Or you could say: 'Do you mean what time is it now or how long does it take to cook?' To which your partner replies patiently: 'No, darling – did you remember to buy the thyme?'

By simply telling your partner the time you'll have taken the question at face value. But by answering the question with a question you'll have dealt with any potential misunderstanding from the outset – and in this case, misunderstanding there certainly was. The question used in this little drama was a forced choice question – one of several specific question types, each of which can be deployed for a particular purpose. In this instance, it helped to defuse a little bit of potential domestic strife. When you use this and other questioning techniques at work, it can save you a deal of trouble from the outset.

Many of the enquiries you deal with will come orally, face-to-face. The possibilities for misunderstandings are endless – accent, articulation, assumptions, all can send you scurrying off in totally the wrong direction, wasting both your time and the enquirer's. But with face-to-face enquiries, you are at least offered lots of clues; most of what we communicate is non-verbal, so you are able to glean what you can from facial expression, eye contact, body language. But you are deprived of these clues when your queries come in by phone, and you have even less to go on when they arrive in written form – by e-mail or text for instance. We'll look at remote enquiry handling in Chapter 2, but right now, let's assume that the enquirer is standing in front of you.

Avoiding misunderstandings

So the first task has to be: always make sure you understand the question. And in almost all cases this means answering a question with a question – a supplementary. There'll be plenty of times when you think the meaning behind the question is obvious. Beware! This happens far less often than you imagine. It has to be as simple a question as 'Where's the toilet?' for you to forgo a supplementary safely. In most other instances, you have to assume that there's more you can learn about the enquirer's needs by questioning a bit further. If you get it wrong, it'll be your fault no matter how unhelpful the enquirer has been. You are the professional, remember, and the enquirer is the amateur.

Just think of all the different types of enquirer you might meet, and the things that could go wrong as a result:

Type 1: The homophone victim

I'm looking for information on migration patterns in whales

means:

I'm looking for information on migration patterns in Wales.

Type 2: The Chinese whisperer

I'm trying to find a song called 'When I Would Sing Under the Ocean'

means:

I'm trying to find a song called 'When I Was King of the Beotians'.

Type 3: The malapropist

Do you have the Electrical Register?

means:

Do you have the electoral register?

Type 4: The generalist

Do you have any books on retailing?

means:

What is Marks & Spencer's current pre-tax profit?

Type 5: The know-all

Where do you keep the New Scientist*?*

means:

I think I saw an article recently about the research that's been done into the health effects of radiation, both from artificial and natural sources, and who's doing it. I don't want to appear ignorant so I'm just going to ask for the latest New Scientist, *which is where I think I saw it.* [In fact, the article appeared in Nature, and was published months ago.]

Type 6: The muddler

Have you got any books on Kew Gardens? That's to say, something on the Crystal Palace, if you can manage it. What would be really helpful, actually, would be the index to the Illustrated London News. *Or, better still, a book on tropical fish.*

means:

I'm doing a project on the Westminster Aquarium.

Type 7: The obsessively secretive

Where's the catalogue?

means (after a lot of tactful questioning):

I know there have been reports in the media that MPs have been accepting cash in return for asking Parliamentary questions, and that one paper has actually named names. I'm very concerned about this because my brother is an MP and he may be involved because he's been asking questions about immigration quotas and he's sponsored by the Strong & Moral Britain Association, which I think has connections with neo-fascist organizations. Can you confirm this, or let me know where its funding comes from? I really need to know because I'm about to become a governor of a school with a large number of Asian children – so I'd also like to find out what obligation there is on school governors to declare other interests, but I don't want to approach the school directly about this in case they start asking awkward questions.

Most of these are based on real enquiries, some are exaggerations. (The last one is almost – but not quite – fictional.) But they all pose real dangers. Rule number one of enquiry answering is that people almost never ask the question to which they really want to know the answer, and there are all sorts of reasons for this.

Disgruntled and unconvinced enquirers

They may not want to bother the staff. It's true, a big public or college library can be a busy place. You can have a queue building up just when Maisie decides to go off for coffee. When you're under pressure, it's always a temptation to take an enquiry at face value and answer the question actually put to you. Resist it! You're almost certain to have a disgruntled customer when they realize that you've sent them somewhere that doesn't actually meet their needs.

They may return to the enquiry desk before too long, complaining that you haven't really helped them. They may try to ask someone else instead – for instance, a passing member of library staff or a fellow student or colleague who happens to be in there. Or they may simply walk out. Whatever happens as a result, it's a waste of everybody's time, and really bad customer relations.

At the very least, you want them to come back and see you if they're not satisfied, so you can do something to limit the damage. But this isn't necessarily all that easy. You may well be busy with another enquirer when they return, so not only will they be growing more and more impatient, but you'll quite possibly be able to see them out of the corner of your eye, which means you might stop paying full attention to the enquirer you're dealing with now – and risk ending up with two disgruntled customers. You may have gone off shift in the meantime, leaving a colleague to placate the enquirer who now has to start all over again with their query. And what if you work in a library where they've abolished the enquiry desk altogether and just have roaming staff? Of course your managers will need to have a procedure for retrieving enquirers who are dissatisfied or want more help – but the best solution is to avoid this happening by asking all the right questions in the first place.

Sceptical enquirers

Equally alarming is the kind of enquirer who lacks confidence in your ability to answer the question. They'd sooner browse themselves, perhaps inefficiently, than risk having their time wasted by you. This kind of enquirer should be sending alarm signals both to you and to your boss. It probably means that they've had bad experiences before – either with your service or somewhere else. Either way, it's up to you to convince them, quickly, that you can help, even if you don't know anything about the subject they are interested in. This doesn't mean trying to pull the wool over their eyes – that's the worst possible tactic. You're bound to get found out, and you'll just reinforce the enquirer's scepticism. There are ways of being helpful, even if you haven't a clue what the enquirer is talking about.

Secretive enquirers

Then there are enquirers who just don't want anyone to know what they're doing. These can be the most infuriating kind. Despite your gentle persuasion, they resolutely refuse to disclose any information that might help you to help them. But you must suppress your urge to get annoyed. That will only make matters worse. They may have excellent reasons for not wanting to give anything away. It might be a colleague applying for a job who doesn't want your current employer to get wind of it. It might be an academic who doesn't want to be beaten to publication by a rival. Or would *you* want everyone to know that you were looking for information on sexually transmitted infections?

Time wasters

Finally, there are time wasters – people who want to burden you with every tiny detail of their investigation, together with the complete life stories of all their sisters, cousins and aunts. Genealogical enquirers frequently fall into this category. You owe it to your other enquirers to steer this type to the point as quickly as possible. They'll try to persuade you that you can't possibly help them without a full understanding of their needs. They may genuinely believe this, or they may simply have time on their hands, and be looking for someone to talk to. Either way, you have to focus them, tactfully.

Equally pernicious are students who try to get you to do their assignments for them. They may come back time and time again trying to get you to look up things that they should really be researching for themselves. This is actually a type of potentially time-wasting activity that you can turn into a benefit. You can seize such opportunities to show them how they can search more efficiently and evaluate the sources they find. (We'll look at smarter searching in Chapter 4.) Sure, coaching them in efficient searching techniques takes time – but at least it's time invested, not time wasted.

Asking the right questions

There are ways of dealing with all these types. You'll need to be approachable, reassuring, discreet, tactful, and frequently, firm as well. Above all, you need a game plan. You have to find out what you need to know by asking questions, and there are several different questioning techniques that you can employ. This is sometimes rather pretentiously referred to as the reference interview, but that implies an inquisitorial formality about the process that can be off-putting for the enquirer. Much better if it comes out as a structured conversation but – here's the crucial bit – with you in charge.

Who, what, when, where, why, how?

'I keep six honest serving men – they taught me all I knew,' said Rudyard Kipling in the *Just So* stories. To answer any enquiry effectively, you need them too. They are the six questions: Who? What? When? Where? Why? How? It's an excellent formula for kicking off your questioning process. This doesn't mean that you necessarily have to ask them all; your enquirer will fill in some of the blanks relatively unprompted and all you have to do is note that information down. But you should certainly address them all, and try to fill in any gaps with your own questioning. The first four – Who? What? When? Where? – are pretty obvious and should provide essential information to enable you to answer the enquiry. The last two – Why? How? – are a bit more subtle.

Firstly, you can use Why? and How? to seek further details that will help you to understand the subject of the enquiry. Remember – there's nothing wrong with not knowing anything about the enquirer's subject. Why should you? That's not your job. But it is your job to help them with sources and search strategies, and for that you do need to understand at least a little about the enquirer's subject. It means that when you begin searching, or helping the enquirer to search, you'll know when you're on the right lines. But you can also use the Why? and How? questions to try to understand the enquirer's reasons for asking. This should enable you to ensure that you provide just the right amount of information, fit for purpose, in the most appropriate form. (We'll come back to this towards the end of the chapter.)

So what do you use these six (or more accurately eight) questions for?

- **Who?** *means* Who are you interested in? (This could be a person, an animal, an organization, a civilization, a society, a movement, a concept.)
- **What?** *means* What are they doing that interests you?
- **When?** *means* Are we dealing with current, recent or historical information?
- **Where?** *means* Which localities, regions or countries do we have to consider?
- **Why?** *firstly means* Why are they doing the thing you're interested in? (This can enable you to start understanding a little of the enquirer's subject.)
- **How?** *firstly means* What methods are they using to do it? (Again, to help you understand more about the subject.)

But in addition:

- **Why?** *can also mean* Why are you, the enquirer, interested in this subject?
- **How?** *can also mean* How do you, the enquirer, want the enquiry handled or the answer delivered?

You wouldn't necessarily always take the questions in this order. (Kipling didn't.) Your enquirer's answers would fill in the blanks for some of them as you went along. Sometimes your questions will seek to elicit more information about the subject the enquirer is interested in, and at other times you will be looking for information on the enquirer's motives and aspirations. But you certainly shouldn't ask them in direct, unvarnished form. A straight 'What do you want?' or – worse – 'Why do you need to know?' sounds combative and inquisitorial and will almost certainly spoil the temporary but intense relationship that you and the enquirer need to have. What you have to do instead is to weave your questions into the structured conversation that is your goal.

Your interrogation strategy

The first thing to say is that it shouldn't come across as an interrogation – nice cop, nasty cop. Nevertheless an interrogation strategy is what you need and it should allow you to do one or other of two things – funnelling or probing. As we'll see in a moment, it will probably be pretty obvious from the enquirer's first question which strategy you need to start with – although you may need to change your strategy as the conversation develops.

Funnelling focuses the enquirer in from the general to the particular. It would probably help with types 4 (the generalist) and 6 (the muddler). However, it can also be an efficient way of dealing with the ambiguities offered by types 1 (the homophone victim), and 5 (the know-all). It's usually the easier of the two techniques to apply because it needn't sound over-inquisitive or threatening. Closed, forced choice and leading questions are all suitable for funnelling operations – although you should bear in mind that each of these techniques carries its own hazards. Forced choice is almost always the most efficient one and we'll come onto the specific questioning techniques in a moment.

Probing seeks further details from the enquirer when you're not at all clear what they want; you might use this strategy to try to find out the context in which the enquirer was thinking. It might help you with types 2 (the Chinese whisperer) or 4 (the generalist), and you'll certainly need to deploy this technique with type 7 (the obsessively secretive). But you have to exercise caution and tact when using it, because it can sound inquisitorial. Open, multiple and hypothetical questions might all help you to probe. On the whole, multiple questions are probably best here – they don't sound so inquisitorial, they show that you're trying to help and taking the enquiry seriously, and they're more likely to put the enquirer at their ease than on their guard.

Six questioning techniques

We've just mentioned some questioning techniques that might help you achieve your strategy, so let's run through all of them now, and the situations in which you might use them.

Open questions invite the enquirer to supply further details without you specifying what additional information would be helpful. You might need to use an open question to deal with a type 4 enquirer (the generalist). Perhaps something like: 'Are you interested in any particular aspect of retailing?' And it may be your only way forward with type 7 (the obsessively secretive) with a response like 'I could give you a hand if you can give me an idea of what subject you're interested in.' However, open questions do have the disadvantage of leaving far too many options open.

Closed questions force the enquirer to give you a yes/no answer. With type 5 (the know-all) you might be tempted to ask, 'Is it the current issue you're looking for?' But, if the know-all runs true to type, the answer will undoubtedly be 'Yes', and you will have learned nothing. So you should use closed questions only when you are pretty certain what the options are. A good time to use a closed question is when you do finally understand what the enquirer really wants and you are literally 'closing the deal'. (We'll come back to agreeing the task to be undertaken a bit later.)

Forced choice questions force the enquirer to choose between alternatives – just two of them. You might ask a type 1 enquirer (the homophone victim), 'Do you mean the sea creatures or the country?' Forced choice is an immensely powerful questioning technique. Firstly, there are only four possible answers: option 1, option 2, both options, or neither. So immediately you are directing the enquiry in ways that are useful to you. Secondly, if you ask someone a forced choice question, they're very likely to leap one way or the other – so it can be a great way of unblocking a secretive enquiry. True, you have to learn to think quickly to come up with two really useful options – but if you can, they'll probably pay dividends both in terms of what you learn and in demonstrating to the enquirer that you're taking a real interest in their needs.

Multiple questions offer the enquirer a range of options (more than two) to choose from when you're really not sure what they want and you need to fish for ideas. Instead of using an open question for type 4 (the generalist), you could try, 'Are you looking for information on retail management, shop design or location, market research, special types of retailer such as food or electrical goods shops – or even one particular retailer?' Of course it's not always easy to think quickly enough to come up with some sensible options

– and you might confuse the enquirer by offering too many. So it's worth considering asking a succession of forced choice questions instead, moving from the general to the particular.

Leading questions lead the enquirer in the direction of the answer you expect. You should only use them when you're 99% certain you do know what the enquirer wants. They can be dangerous, because they impose your assumptions on the enquirer's request, when you really need to be certain that you haven't made any false assumptions. With type 1, you might ask, 'So it's statistics on their movements that you're looking for then?' Your enquirer might answer 'Yes', and be quite right. But you still don't know whether it's 'whales' or 'Wales'.

Hypothetical questions attempt to glean further information by putting a hypothetical situation to the enquirer. As with multiple questions, you have to be able to think on your feet to come up quickly with a sensible hypothetical scenario. But it might be your only hope with type 6 (the muddler). You're not allowed to ask the forbidden question: 'What do you really want?' Put this way, it sounds aggressive and suspicious and sends out the wrong signals to the enquirer. But you can put the same question in a hypothetical form by asking 'What would your ideal answer look like?'

Is there a questioning 'magic bullet'? Probably not. But perhaps forced choice questioning comes close because of its diagnostic capabilities. When your optician puts two lenses in front of you in succession and asks: 'Better 1 or 2?' that's a classic forced choice question, enabling the specialist to narrow down the options based on responses from the layperson. But all these questioning techniques have their value at different times. And when you're finally deciding how to set about answering the enquiry or helping the enquirer to answer it – and keep down your panic at the same time – then the magic bullet is undoubtedly the hypothetical question that you ask yourself. (We'll come back to that in Chapter 3.)

Does all this really work?

That's enough of the theory. Let's see how all this might work for the questions to which our enquirers really wanted answers.

Type 1: The homophone victim

I'm looking for information on migration patterns in whales	Who? What? When? Where? Why? How?	Interrogation strategy	Questioning technique
Ah, so we need to be looking in the zoology section?	**Who** are we looking for?	Probing	Closed
Oh, sorry – you mean people moving around Wales?	**What** are they doing?	Probing	Closed
Do you mean things like how they travel to work, or what they do when they move house or where they come from?	**How** are they doing it?	Probing	Multiple
Is it just movements within the country, or from outside as well?	**Where** do we have to consider?	Funnelling	Forced choice
Are you looking just for movements now – or back over a period?	**When** do we have to consider?	Funnelling	Forced choice
Are you looking for information on why people move, or do you just need the figures?	**Why** do you need the information?	Funnelling	Forced choice
I'm looking for information on migration patterns in Wales.			

Verdict: Once you've got over the initial misunderstanding, you should be able to get all the way with this enquiry – it's precise and specific.

Type 2: The Chinese whisperer

I'm trying to find a song called 'When I Would Sing Under the Ocean'	Who? What? When? Where? Why? How?	Interrogation strategy	Questioning technique
Right; have you any idea who sings it, or who it's written by?	**Who** are we looking for?	Funnelling	Forced choice
I'm afraid I can't find a song of that title. How did you come to hear of it?	**How** can we take this enquiry forward?	Probing	Open
Oh, you heard it on the radio. Can you remember which station or programme?	**Where** did you hear it?	Funnelling	Open
Was it a pop song or something more traditional?	**When** might it have been written?	Funnelling	Forced choice
Oh, so it was a baritone solo and you think it might have come from an opera or musical?	**What** kind of song was it?	Funnelling	Leading
Since it's not showing up in any of our musical sources, perhaps the title's slightly different – so shall we try to think of some other way of identifying it?	**Why** aren't we finding it, when the enquiry seems so straightforward?	Probing	Leading
I'm trying to find a song called 'When I Would Sing Under the Ocean'. [But the title is probably wrong.]			

Verdict: At this stage in your questioning, you're not going to find out what you're really supposed to be looking for because the enquirer has got the question wrong. As far as you're concerned, you're still looking for a song called 'When I Would Sing Under the Ocean' but just not finding it anywhere. However, several things that emerged during your questioning should help you to understand the challenges you face – particularly the fact that the enquirer discovered the title aurally. This should arouse your Chinese Whisper suspicions. Meanwhile you now have lots of ideas for places to try: the radio station that played the song, guides to opera and musicals, even asking the enquirer to hum the tune so you can look it up in a dictionary of musical themes or on a music finder website or app.

Type 3: The malapropist

Do you have the Electrical Register?	Who? What? When? Where? Why? How?	Interrogation strategy	Questioning technique
I'm sorry, I can't find a directory or website with that name. Is it electricians you're looking for?	**Who** are you looking for?	Probing	Closed
Oh, I beg your pardon, I must have misheard – it's the voters' list you need. The local one or for some other area?	**Where** are you interested in?	Funnelling	Forced choice
And I presume you want the current one?	**When** do you want to cover?	Funnelling	Leading
Are you just looking up a specific address, or do you need to browse through?	**What** kind of information do you need to find?	Probing	Forced choice
So you're looking for people with particular surnames. Is this because you're trying to trace someone?	**Why** do you need the information?	Probing	Closed
There might be other kinds of source that could do the job better – websites that can help you trace people, genealogical sites – even social networking sites. What form would you like the information in?	**How** do you want the enquiry handled?	Probing	Open
Do you have the electoral register? [But is that really the best source to use for the purpose?]			

Verdict: In this instance, we've taken the line of questioning much further than was necessary to answer the enquiry initially posed – even without the misunderstanding. But it does go to show just how much may lie behind even the most apparently simple request. Once you've realized the enquirer's initial mistake, you will need to respond tactfully so as to spare them any embarrassment – and at the very least you will need to confirm that it is the current register for your local area that they want; you shouldn't just assume that it is. But in any case, it's beginning to sound as if the Electoral Register may not be the most efficient way of meeting the enquirer's needs – so it might be worth taking the questioning even further, while starting to suggest possible solutions at the same time.

Type 4: The generalist

Do you have any books on retailing?	Who? What? When? Where? Why? How?	Interrogation strategy	Questioning technique
Yes, plenty – and other kinds of information source as well. Are you interested in retail management, shop design or location, market research, special types of retailer such as food or electrical goods shops – or even one particular retailer?	**What** aspect of retailing are you interested in?	Funnelling	Multiple
Ah, so it is one retailer. Are you looking for financial information or news on the company's activities?	**What** particular activity are you interested in?	Funnelling	Forced choice
So you just need the latest accounts?	**When** are you interested in?	Funnelling	Closed
Just the company's UK business, or does it have worldwide operations as well?	**Where** do we need to consider?	Funnelling	Forced choice
Is it detailed data for investment purposes, or just a brief financial profile for information?	**Why** do you need this information?	Funnelling	Forced choice
Do you need to be able to download the figures into a spreadsheet so you can manipulate them?	**How** do you want the information presented?	Funnelling	Closed
What is Marks & Spencer's current pre-tax profit? [No – you still don't know which company the enquirer wants.]			

Verdict: Enquirers can be extraordinarily secretive about money matters, so it's probably wise to have delayed the crucial question: 'Which retailer is it?' Even so, you haven't wasted your time. There is an enormous amount of business information available and it's easy to bury an enquirer under a deluge of semi-relevant information. So it's worth funnelling to find out precisely what they want without being too specific. By this time, maybe they'll have gained sufficient confidence in you to divulge the name. Or perhaps that's an over-optimistic scenario!

Type 5: The know-all

Where do you keep the *New Scientist*?	Who? What? When? Where? Why? How?	Interrogation strategy	Questioning technique
The current issue is on the display racks, but we have back issues as well if you're looking for something specific?	**What** are you looking for?	Probing	Open (by implication)
So you'd like to check some back issues as well. How far back would you like to go?	**When** do you think the article appeared?	Funnelling	Open
Are you looking for a particular article that you know appeared in the *New Scientist* or are you just looking for information on a particular topic?	**Why** do you need the *New Scientist* specifically?	Probing	Forced choice
So it's information on radiation risks. If you can't spot the article you remembered from the *New Scientist*, would you like to check elsewhere as well?	**How** do you want to progress your enquiry?	Probing	Closed
Probably the most efficient way to find further information on this topic would be to use our discovery platform for articles that might have appeared in other scientific titles that we have access to. For example, *Nature* covers the same sort of subjects as *New Scientist*.	**Where** else would you like to search?	Probing	Leading (by implication)
I think I saw an article recently about the research that's been done into the health effects of radiation, both from artificial and natural sources, and who's doing it. I don't want to appear ignorant so I'm just going to ask for the latest New Scientist, *which is where I think I saw it.* [In fact, the article appeared in Nature, and was published months ago.]			

Verdict: This may seem like going to enormous lengths to deal with what appears initially to be a very straightforward query. But it turned out not to be straightforward, and your tactful probing may have prevented the enquirer from leaving in a disgruntled mood after failing to find the article in the current *New Scientist*.

Type 6: The muddler

Have you got any books on Kew Gardens? That's to say, something on the Crystal Palace, if you can manage it. What would be really helpful, actually, would be the index to the *Illustrated London News*. Or, better still, a book on tropical fish.	Who? What? When? Where? Why? How?	Interrogation strategy	Questioning technique
That's a wide range of topics; is there a common factor?	**Who** (or what subject) are you interested in?	Probing	Open
Where do the tropical fish come into it?	**Why** did you mention them?	Funnelling	Open
So it's aquariums. Victorian ones?	**When** would this be?	Funnelling	Closed
And is it particularly London you're interested in?	**Where** are these aquariums?	Funnelling	Closed
So you want to concentrate on one aquarium; which one would that be?	**How** do you want the enquiry to proceed?	Funnelling	Open
I'm doing a project on the Westminster Aquarium.			

Verdict: Like type 4, this is probably an over-optimistic scenario. The true muddler would likely go on muddling for some time before giving you the opportunity to start funnelling. But one advantage that muddlers offer over generalists or the obsessively secretive is that they do at least give you plenty of clues to work on – and in this instance one huge anomaly which it's really worth focusing on: the fish.

Type 7: The obsessively secretive

Where's the catalogue?	Who? What? When? Where? Why? How?	Interrogation strategy	Questioning technique
We have a public catalogue which you can use here or access online, but it only covers the books and we have plenty of other resources as well – journals, news media, directories, guides to websites.	**How** can I help you?	Probing	Multiple (by implication)
So it's something in the newspapers?	**What** sort of information do you need?	Probing	Closed
Do you know roughly when?	**When** should we start looking?	Funnelling	Closed
I can show you one or two news sites that might help. What's the subject you're interested in?	**What** kind of information do you need?	Funnelling	Open

Continued on the next page

Type 7: The obsessively secretive *(continued)*

Where's the catalogue?	Who? What? When? Where? Why? How?	Interrogation strategy	Questioning technique
So it's the cash-for-questions affair – how would you like to narrow the search down after that?	**How** would you like the enquiry to proceed?	Funnelling	Open
Ah, if it's a particular organization you want, its website is more likely to help you.	**Who** are you looking for?	Funnelling	Closed (by implication)
So its website doesn't tell you how it's funded. We could see if we could try to find some articles or blog postings on it.	**What** is this organization doing for funds?	Funnelling	Closed (by implication again)
So it's the race relations aspect you're interested in? For any particular purpose?	**Why** do you need this information?	Probing	Open
So it's school governorships? Sorry, I don't understand the connection with the cash-for-questions issue.	**Why** do you need to know this?	Probing	Open (by implication)
It's a family connection? So it's a question of possible conflict of interest?	**How** are the two issues linked?	Probing	Closed
So we're looking for something like the rules for school governors?	**How** do you want the subject handled?	Probing	Closed
Cash for Parliamentary questions ... Strong & Moral Britain Association ... neo-fascist organizations ... funding ... school governors ... declarations of interest.			

Verdict: Like type 6, this is a somewhat compressed scenario. It would probably take a lot of very tactful questioning to elicit all the aspects of this complex and sensitive affair. Restricting your questioning initially to sources, delivery media and searching techniques, as opposed to the specific information required, will probably reassure your enquirer. Then you can use your demonstration of how the source or delivery medium works to find out more about what your enquirer actually wants – perhaps by means of a succession of step-by-step closed questions, a technique resorted to frequently in this scenario.

If you look back, you'll see that a few of the 'questions' in these little scenarios aren't actually questions at all. But they still invite an answer nevertheless, and sometimes posing a question as a statement can keep the encounter reassuringly non-inquisitorial. And you may also have spotted that there are no hypothetical questions here at all. To be frank, you need to be pretty desperate to ask a hypothetical question – maybe something along the lines of: 'If we found you information on so-and-so, would that be helpful?' But to ask a hypothetical you have to make something up, thereby moving the whole process away from the realm of fact and towards fiction, so it's to be avoided if possible. You may have no choice if you can get nowhere with the muddler or the obsessively secretive enquirer – but avoid making hypothetical questions part of your regular interrogation strategy if you possibly can.

(Remember, though, you are going to need the hypothetical questioning technique for the next stage of the process – covered in Chapter 3.)

Agreeing the task

As you can see from these examples, some of your questions come out as requests for further information, others as reactions to information received. That's how it usually happens in real life; the responses to either type will help you to fill in more of the blanks. You'll have been taking notes during your structured conversation with the enquirer – won't you? (We'll deal with record keeping in detail in Chapter 2.) So now is the time to repeat back to them what you think they want you to do – something like:

- So we're looking for figures on how people have moved into, out of and within Wales between the 2001 and 2011 Censuses?
- So we're looking for a song that's a baritone solo that you probably heard on BBC Radio 2 last Sunday, with a title something like 'When I Would Sing Under the Ocean'?
- So browsing through the current electoral register for this area might be a useful starting point, but we're also going to locate other sources that may help you to trace the names you're looking for more efficiently?
- So we just need a single figure – Marks & Spencer's latest pre-tax profit?
- So we're looking for information on who's doing research into the health risks of artificial and natural radiation, and it's worth searching elsewhere if we don't find the article you remember from *New Scientist*?
- So we're looking for anything we can find on the Westminster Aquarium, which was demolished some time in the late 19th or early 20th century?
- So we need: something on the funding of the Strong & Moral Britain Association; information on whatever rules affect school governors; and it

would help to have something from the news media on the cash-for-questions affair?

What you have by this stage is an implied contract with your enquirer. It may not be legally enforceable, but that's its function nevertheless. If you deviate from it without consulting your enquirer again, then you can no longer guarantee that you're meeting their needs, and you're almost certainly not making the most efficient use of your time either. (We'll come back to occasions when you may need to deviate from the original request in Chapter 5.) And note the use of the word 'we'. It doesn't matter whether you're simply helping your enquirer to locate sources, advising them on using those sources efficiently, or undertaking the complete research project yourself – this is your problem now, as well as your enquirer's, and it is only good customer relations to make that clear by involving yourself in it. And that includes not simply helping them find the answer, but helping them find it in a form that's useful to them.

Not too little, not too much

Pretty much right up to the end of the 20th century, if you wanted to find something out you usually had to be content with whatever you could glean from a large but strictly limited number of proprietary (and usually charged-for) sources – whether printed, online or published in a portable digital medium such as a CD-ROM. If these didn't yield what you wanted, there wasn't a lot more you could do with documentary sources. You had to start casting round looking for experts in the field or else give up and be content with at best a second-rate answer.

How things have changed! Almost all those proprietary sources are still there – and usually available in the form of a much wider range of products – plus a great many more charged-for services besides. And to all those you have to add information from hundreds of thousands of potentially relevant websites – many of them free – as well as possibly millions of blog posts and billions of comments on social media. When an enquirer asks you 'Get me everything you've got on…' the time is not far off when you're going to be able to do just that. And that's almost certainly too much.

So the last stage in your questioning is to find out more or less how much information your enquirer needs, and of what kind – and this is where your secondary Why? and How? questions come in: 'Why do you need to know this?' and 'How do you want the enquiry handled or the answer delivered?' If you're actually doing the work on the enquirer's behalf, you have the tools to bombard them with information, but you're not helping them if you do that, because they're looking to you not only to find the information they need but also to help them filter it, so that they end up with just enough to do whatever they want to do – no more, no less. The same applies if you're simply advising – getting a student started on a research project for example. They may be doing the work, but they still expect you to guide them to the most appropriate sources for their purpose.

So you could simply ask an open question: 'How much information do you need?' But you might not get a very precise answer; 'Whatever you can find' doesn't really help you very much. Also some enquirers might feel daunted by the task of trying to imagine for themselves what the final answer might look like. That's your job – and we're going to return to it in some detail in Chapter 3. So a multiple question might be better – something like: 'Do you just want a few main points in note form, or a page or so of information, or something like an article, or a complete book?'

This of course assumes that you have a fair idea of the form in which the information is likely to appear. But if it's a highly technical subject, or the enquirer has used terminology that is unfamiliar to you, you might not know what to expect. So a third possibility might be to put the hypothetical question: 'What would your ideal answer look like?' This again puts the onus back on the enquirer, so it's to be avoided if at all possible. But it may be your only hope if your enquirer has really taken you into totally unfamiliar territory. (Whether or not you ask the *enquirer* this question, it's an absolutely crucial one that you need to ask *yourself* – as we shall see in Chapter 3.)

Information for a purpose

People rarely want information merely to satisfy their curiosity – they almost always need it for a purpose. An academic about to embark on a piece of ground-breaking new research may indeed need to know everything that's been discovered on a particular topic – but that almost certainly still only means everything in the academic and professional literature, and blog posts or tweets only from acknowledged specialists in the field. A practitioner, with a specific problem to solve, may also want to draw on the same body of specialist literature and seek out comment from the same experts – but may be happy with a good selection of practical solutions to that problem, irrespective of how much more might have been written about it in theory. And yet they may both have started by saying: 'Get me everything you've got on . . .'

Then there are student assignments. However much you may privately regret a student's lack of curiosity, or deplore the narrow focus of a curriculum that forces this attitude upon them, you have to be realistic about it. You're not helping the hapless student or school child at all if you don't take a pragmatic approach. The fact is that they need enough information to allow them to get a good mark, and once they've got that, they can't afford the time to go browsing for more information because they've probably got more assignments or homework projects coming up to deadline too. So help them find what they want, and then when they've got enough – stop.

And of course, you have to know just how much help to give. Teachers and lecturers are notorious at handing out projects with no thought whatsoever for the ease or difficulty of the research involved. You can easily be faced by two children from the same school class, one of whom wants to do a project on dinosaurs and the other on 14th-century Byzantine art, where the teacher appears to have given no thought whatever to the possibility that these might not represent tasks of equal difficulty. In these circumstances, you clearly need to get the dinosaur child started quickly, and devote the bulk of your attention to the Byzantine one.

Retirement hobbyists, on the other hand, may be operating at the opposite extreme. They're delighted with every additional snippet of detail you can provide – even if they've read it in a dozen other places already. The danger here, of course, is that – in the nicest possible way – they can be terrible time-wasters. Whether you actually get carried along by their enthusiasm, or simply can't shake them off, you have to be systematic about your choice of sources to help them too – and the order of priority in which you suggest them. In both these cases – the student and the hobbyist – the aim is to help your enquirer become self-sufficient as rapidly as possible: to give them something to read, and get them settled down reading it.

Getting answers to these **Why?** and **How?** questions may require quite a lot of care on your part. You may need both to probe and funnel to find out whether your enquirer is operating at postgraduate level or starting from a position of total ignorance. No one wants to be thought ignorant, and it's only human nature for people to pretend to greater knowledge than they actually have. So you must use the answers to your Who? What? When? Where? Why? How? questions to judge how much your enquirer knows already. Again, this determines the types of source you use or recommend. A layperson asking about varicose veins may just want a medical dictionary, a home health guide or a health advice web page, but a student doctor probably wants articles from the clinical press. An enquirer who asks you for textbooks about anatomy may be a paramedic studying fractures, but may equally be an art student studying life drawing.

Finding out how long you've got

Finally, you have to agree a deadline. Often, this will be 'now'. The enquirer will be standing there, and they'll want you to point them in the right direction straight away. But if the enquiry has come in by phone, e-mail or text, or if the enquirer is going to leave now and let you get on with it, you need to be quite clear when they need the answer. So don't take 'As soon as possible' or 'It's urgent' for an answer. 'As soon as possible' could mean next year from your point of view, and urgency can be measured in minutes or days. So politely pin your enquirer down to a date, and a time too if the deadline is tight.

Admittedly this isn't always easy when you're dealing with a senior colleague in your organization or a peppery academic in your college, or even sometimes an impatient and intimidating member of the public. So be prepared to explain why you need to agree a firm deadline: so that you can provide as full a response as is feasible within the timescale. And if you think that timescale is unrealistically short, try not to say: 'Can't be done.' Keep it positive. Explain that you will only be able to provide a limited answer in that time, and invite your enquirer to extend the deadline. More often than not, you'll find that they are able to give you more time. (We'll deal with meeting deadlines in Chapter 5.)

Coming next – when the enquirer's not there . . .

We've discovered that plenty can go wrong with even the apparently simplest of enquiries, we've found out a bit about how to avoid some of these pitfalls and learned that good customer care is an essential part of the process. But that's when you actually have the enquirer standing in front of you. When the enquirer's at the other end of the phone, or e-mailing or texting in, even more things can go wrong and maintaining good customer relations becomes even more vital. So in Chapter 2, we'll look at some of the things you need to think about when dealing with enquirers remotely.

To recap . . .

■ Beware of the pitfalls presented by homophone victims, Chinese whisperers, malapropists, generalists, know-alls, muddlers and the obsessively secretive.

■ Look for answers to the questions Who? What? When? Where? Why? How?

■ Be ready to funnel or probe as appropriate, and employ open, closed, forced choice, multiple, leading or hypothetical questions.

■ Reach firm agreement about what you will do for the enquirer, and in how much detail.

■ Make sure you agree a clear deadline for the work.

CHAPTER 2

Flying blind

Why remote enquiry handling is different

In this chapter you'll find out how to:

- **deal with enquiries by phone, e-mail or text**
- **avoid even more misunderstandings**
- **keep your enquirer on side**
- **get into the habit of good record keeping.**

'Please listen carefully to the following three options: To annoy the customer, press 1; to waste everybody's time, press 2; to lose business, press 3.'

Up to now we've been assuming that your encounter with the enquirer has been face-to-face; we've learned quite a bit about what can go wrong if you don't anticipate potential misunderstandings and be ready to deal with them before they happen. But at least you've had plenty of other clues – besides what you and the enquirer actually say to one another – to reinforce your suspicion that things might be going wrong.

You might detect a pained expression flitting across the enquirer's face as they realize that they're not getting their needs across. They might be drumming their fingers with impatience at the lack of progress, or standing with their arms akimbo as if to demand an explanation. Or they might be avoiding eye contact with you – indicating, perhaps, that they have something to hide or, worse, that they don't have confidence in your ability to help them.

When you observe 'tells' like this in your enquirer's facial expression or body language, it does at least give you an opportunity to take remedial action. But when you can't see, and sometimes can't even hear, your enquirer, you have none of these clues to draw upon, and that means that even more things can go wrong than we encountered in Chapter 1.

As the quote at the start of this chapter indicates, call centres tend to have a pretty terrible reputation. But when you do encounter a good one, you'll find it leads the way in high-quality customer service. That lesson applies just as much to information services as it does to those provided by banks, travel firms or IT helpdesks. Like them or loathe them, people are expecting more and more of the services they need to be delivered remotely.

They may be students who want instant guidance from their university resource centre before embarking on their own literature search online. They could be colleagues or superiors in some distant office in your organization for whom time is money. Or they might be users who simply want to check that there's going to be something useful for them to look at before they come into their local library. Whatever their needs, you must be ready to satisfy them whether they choose to communicate by phone, e-mail, text or instant messaging.

Once again, there's a formal phrase that pulls all of these practices together: virtual reference. It can encompass videoconferencing and Voice Over Internet Protocol (VOIP) as well as the media mentioned above. But the actual communication medium is less important than the tactics you deploy when using it to ensure that your relationship with the enquirer runs smoothly – and that's all about being aware that when you can't see or hear each other, you're actually deprived of most of the clues that we take for granted when dealing with people face-to-face.

Can't see, can't hear – the risk of misunderstanding, even offence

Let's get the bad news out of the way first. All sorts of extra things can go wrong when you're dealing with enquirers remotely, and here are some of the reasons why…

Opening hours

Face-to-face: When they have to come to your building to use your services, users do generally appreciate that you have opening hours and other times when you're closed, and they'll expect to see a notice outside saying what those times are.

Remote: As far as telephone or online customers are concerned, you're never closed. After all, you're not just providing remote services for their convenience; it's also benefitting you in terms of saved premises costs – so the least you can do in return is be open all hours. You may not actually like the idea of working 24 hours a day, but you need to be aware that that may be what your enquirer expects.

Response time

Face-to-face: When the enquirer's actually with you, they can see you're working and are generally prepared to wait a bit while you deal with people ahead of them in the queue.

Remote: When they can't see that you're working hard – either on their enquiry or somebody else's while they wait their turn – there's a tendency for remote enquirers to assume that you're on a permanent tea break from the moment you hang up the phone after taking their enquiry to the time you do finally return their call. And that's not even considering the time they may have spent waiting to get through to you in the first place – so you might find you have a disgruntled customer on your hands before you even start.

Customer loyalty

Face-to-face: If an enquirer has bothered to make the journey to your premises in the first place, they're likely to stick with you even if you're having difficulty satisfying their requirements. They've already invested time in coming to see you, and they'll have to use up even more time if they decide to give up on you and travel somewhere else – with no guarantee of faring any better when they do.

Remote: It may only have taken a few minutes for the customer to put their enquiry into an e-mail, or to phone or text you – so if they decide they're not getting good service, it's only going to take a few minutes more to phone somewhere else instead or click on a different link. Why wait if they're not happy?

Service quality

Face-to-face: Hopefully, an enquirer should get service of the same high quality wherever they choose to go – and that includes being given an answer of comparable quality no matter who they ask. But if they feel that they're not getting good service, it's still probably less hassle to stay where they are and persevere, rather than perhaps waste time going elsewhere in search of a better answer.

Remote: If an enquirer doesn't like the answer you've provided, and feels they can get a better one elsewhere, it doesn't matter how hard you've worked on their behalf. It's so easy and quick for them to try somewhere else that they'll quite likely do just that.

Searching time and effort

Face-to-face: If you have the enquirer with you, you can give them some initial advice and then leave them browsing print materials or looking through search results while you deal with somebody else. Your enquirer can see that you're not slacking, and hopefully also knows that they can ask you for further help whenever they need it.

Remote: If you're dealing with an enquiry that has come in by phone or text-based media, you really have to do all the searching, and the selection and rejection of possible sources, on the enquirer's behalf. It's no good telling the enquirer 'Oh, you'll have to come in', because what's the point of offering a remote service if they have to do that? Instead, you'll probably have to do a lot more work on the enquirer's behalf, and they'll probably already have done the simple searching themselves.

Cross-selling and up-selling

First of all, a quick explanation of these two terms. **Cross-selling** is when you ask for one thing and the provider tries to sell you something else of comparable value at the same time. You might go into your local coffee shop just to buy a pastry, and the server asks: 'Would you like a drink with that?' That's cross-selling. **Up-selling** is when you've bought something of a certain value and the provider tries to sell you something of higher value. They might be trying to persuade you to come off a pay-as-you-go tariff on your mobile phone, for example, and go onto a longer-term subscription plan instead. If they succeed in persuading you to change, that's up-selling.

Now you may think that none of this applies to you running an information service. You're not actually selling anything, and you've got a captive market in any case. You'd probably be wrong on both counts.

Firstly, even if no money changes hands with each enquiry, someone's still paying you to provide the service you do. Whether it's a student paying high tuition fees (and probably incurring long-term debt in the process), a colleague or superior who may be inclined to see the corporate information unit as an overhead rather than a profit centre, or simply a member of the public who pays their local taxes, it's your enquirer who pays in the end – and quite reasonably expects value for money.

And you haven't got a captive market any more either, even if you ever did. Your student can try the professional association of which they're a student member, your colleague or superior can use their professional social network to ask one of their peers, and your member of the public can simply go on the web.

So with that possible misconception out of the way . . .

Face-to-face: Someone who visits your premises in person can browse around while they're waiting for someone to help them, and perhaps find the very thing they need by serendipity – maybe even something better than you thought to offer them.

Remote: Apart from browsing through whatever you provide on your website, a remote enquirer is entirely in your hands when it comes to ideas for places to look. If they've already looked on the web unsuccessfully, it's up to you to come up with higher value sources to try, and to contribute your own expertise as a professional searcher. Not to mention seizing any opportunity you can to persuade your student to come on a library induction course, your colleague or superior to sign up for your current awareness service, or your member of the public to attend a local event that relates to their interests.

Non-verbal clues

Face-to-face: As the opening scenario of this chapter suggests, we get most of the clues as to how our brief but intense relationship with the enquirer is going not from the words they use but from how they appear to be reacting. It's probably not wise to try to put actual figures on it, but as a general rule it's safe to assume that we gain only a fraction of the clues we need from what the enquirer actually says, and a great deal more from how they say it. If you doubt this, just repeat a simple sentence over and over – 'I hope you can help me', for example – and try putting the emphasis on each word in turn. You'll probably be astonished at how your perception of the mood of the enquirer changes each time.

However, it's generally agreed that we can learn even more about how the enquirer's feeling from their body language, facial expression and eye contact than from all the other clues put together – and take remedial action if necessary. So when you're dealing with an enquirer face-to-face, don't just focus on your workstation or keep your nose buried in your notes. Look at them as much as possible; it will tell you a lot.

Remote: On the phone, you can hear what your enquirer is saying and the tone of voice they're using, but you can't see if they're secretly getting impatient or losing confidence in you. They may sound as if they're being patient, but may actually be silently rolling their eyes in exasperation. And if they're e-mailing or texting, you don't even have tone of voice to go on. Even if the words look restrained and polite, you have no idea what emphasis the enquirer is putting on them – and as we've already seen, that emphasis can change the character of a message dramatically.

Keeping your remote enquirer on side

Right – that's the bad news dealt with. Now we need to consider how to avoid all these potential pitfalls.

The first thing to say is that everything we learned in Chapter 1 applies here too – even more so. Your initial interrogation strategy – whether to funnel or probe – and the questioning techniques you use are both essential because with a remote enquirer you have even less time and opportunity to discover what they really want.

Why? Because unless it's a very straightforward enquiry, you're quite likely to need to take the enquirer's details and then promise to call (or e-mail or text) them back. That means that you absolutely must gather all the information you need during that first phone call or in the first rapid exchange of e-mails or texts.

When the enquirer is physically with you, you do have the opportunity to ask further questions that you may not have thought of at the beginning without risking their becoming too impatient, because they can see you're working hard on their behalf. But when the enquirer is somewhere else, and perhaps wondering what on earth you're doing all this time, each time you phone or e-mail them again they're going to think you're finally coming back with the answer. They're going to become understandably more and more impatient if you need to ask yet another question that you should have thought to ask in the first place. So your Who? What? When? Where? Why?

How?, your discussion of what they need the information for, how much detail they want and how they want the answer delivered, and your agreement on a deadline for the job, are as vital as ever.

And to all the risks of misunderstanding that we looked at in Chapter 1, you have to add things like noisy phone connections, the signal breaking up, the call being dropped because the enquirer's train has just gone into a tunnel – any of which can either add to the risk of mishearing, or interrupt your thought processes. And when it comes to text-based media, you have the additional hazard of misleading typos. If someone e-mails or texts you asking how they can become a qualified diver in France, how are you to know that they actually mean a qualified *driver* – unless you ask a supplementary question? And when you do think to ask it, how can you be sure that your message doesn't come across as flippant or patronizing?

So following are some thoughts about remote enquiry etiquette.

When the phone rings…

This may seem counter-intuitive, but don't snatch it up immediately. (Of course the other principle applies too: don't let it ring interminably.) Even though they've initiated the call, an enquirer often uses the ringing time to gather their thoughts. They may even be taking the pessimistic but often all too justified view that their call is *unlikely* to be answered with any degree of promptitude, so they might as well put the ringing time to good use by thinking what they're going to say.

So if you do snatch the phone up before it's even had time to finish its first ring, you'll quite possibly be dealing with a surprised and confused enquirer who doesn't actually hear the first few words you say and has to ask you to repeat them. If you let the phone ring a couple of times before picking it up, you're much more likely to have a composed and attentive enquirer on your hands.

Your phone style

When you answer the phone, what are you going to say? Do you start with 'Good morning', 'Hello' or 'Hi'? Do you say the full name of your organization or just use its abbreviation or acronym and hope that the caller will know they've come through to the right place? Remember, you can't see if your enquirer looks stiff and formal, or relaxed and laid-back. So you need to agree (with your team or management if appropriate) what form of initial greeting you'll use, neither too formal nor too informal. At this point, what you say on the phone *is* your organization's branding, just as much as its signage, stationery, publicity material and website are.

But that doesn't mean reading from a script. That's almost certain to sound forced and robotic, and it also sends out the message that the enquirer's requirements are going to have to match your procedures, instead of you being flexible in meeting the enquirer's needs. Using a script can also put you at a disadvantage, because you have to stick to the prescribed words while the enquirer can say anything they like in response, forcing you to fight with one hand tied behind your back. Remember, this is supposed to be a structured conversation, but with you (tactfully) in charge.

Sometimes you do need to include specific information for legal purposes – a disclaimer saying that you're not qualified to give legal or medical advice, a reassurance that the enquiry will be dealt with in confidence, or a warning that the call may be recorded for training purposes. Again, if at all possible, it's best not to have to read this from a script; try to get clearance to use your own common-sense form of words, based on clear guidelines about the information that you have to convey.

Speaking speed and clarity

Your enquirer is going to need a little more time to adjust to your voice, your accent and what you're saying when on the phone – and they may be taking notes too. With no visual signals, the voice is all you and the enquirer have, so what you say and how you say it become all the more important. So speak at a slightly steadier pace than you would perhaps need to face-to-face. BBC reporters use a rule of thumb of three words a second. It's slightly slower than normal conversation, but it's not as slow as dictation speed, and a good benchmark to adopt, with practice.

And just in case you're worrying, this has nothing to do with your accent. Your accent is special, it's your precious legacy, it's what makes you 'you'. So celebrate your accent – but still make sure you speak steadily and clearly.

International callers and enquirers not using their first language

Which brings us on neatly to enquirers and *their* accents. Firstly, if you think someone may be calling from abroad, it might be courteous to help keep their costs down by offering to continue the conversation by e-mail (or possibly text). Or if you use VOIP, you could offer to call them back using that usually cheaper if not actually free medium. If you do suggest this, and they agree, then it's pretty essential to resume the conversation in the new medium more or less straight away. If you don't the enquirer may think you're just fobbing them off. One incidental benefit of using e-mail is that it may make it easier to understand what the enquirer wants if they have a strong accent on the phone – but that shouldn't be a reason for suggesting continuing the conversation in a text-based medium, just a bonus.

If you are having difficulty understanding someone's accent on the phone it can be a real challenge, but there are some things you can do about it nevertheless. Think carefully, for example, about the kinds of questions you use. Closed and forced choice questions, for example, require the enquirer to respond to your suggestions rather than having to frame sentences and recall vocabulary for themselves. However, in order to ask such questions you need to have listened to at least some of the enquirer's requirements to begin with.

If you try all this and still have problems understanding, risking wasting the enquirer's time as a result, you could claim that the connection is noisy, or that you're having difficulty hearing. It has to be said that this isn't a particularly ethical approach if it's not true, but it may be justified if it enables you to start helping the enquirer while keeping the relationship positive.

And finally, show the enquirer some courtesy yourself. As well as speaking more steadily, try to use short sentences with few subordinate clauses. But don't fall into the trap of using excessively simple words, and certainly don't shout – that's just patronizing.

Laconic or loquacious enquirers

Even if you and your enquirer do share a native language, that still doesn't necessarily mean that they're going to make their wishes clear and unambiguous. Some people may provide very clipped and unhelpful answers over the phone, followed by an awkward silence while you decide how to respond (and silences on the phone seem much longer than silences face-to-face). Others might ramble on without giving you an opportunity to ask supplementary questions because they're unable to see any gestures that might indicate that you would like to intervene.

Once again, you can deploy different questioning techniques to meet each situation. For laconic enquirers, open questions might encourage them to expand on their requirements, or multiple questions might induce them to opt for one or more choices. Loquacious enquirers might be brought to heel with closed or forced choice questions to help them focus.

Fielding complaints

It's a depressing thing to have to think about, but there's always the possibility that the next phone call you take is going to be a complaint. There is even a suggestion that people who initially enquired by e-mail will subsequently complain by phone – but whether that's true or not, the fact is that you get none of the clues that someone's unhappy with your service before the phone rings and they start complaining at you.

When you're dealing with a complainer face-to-face, you're quite likely to have seen them approach you with a determined expression and tension in their body, so you do at least have a second or two to get into complaint-deflection mode. But when you pick up the phone, it comes at you without warning.

One common complaint comes from the caller who claims they were speaking to someone but got cut off. This is a tricky one; it may be true or it may be a ploy. Obviously you can use some of the questioning techniques we discussed in Chapter 1 to try to discover who they might have been speaking to before and hopefully put them back to that person. But if that's not possible it means that the complainer becomes your responsibility, and it's sensible customer relations to give them some sort of priority, if only for the sake of sending them away placated instead of disgruntled.

But complaints can actually come in all manner of guises. So the first piece of advice is: always assume that the next call is going to be a complaint. Although this may sound a dismal approach to adopt, the reality is that most of your calls are not going to be complaints (unless you're very unlucky or your organization has done something to annoy a lot of people) so immediately you can start off feeling happier about things than you did before you picked up. And if you do find yourself having to calm an irate caller or stand up to someone who's trying to bully you over the phone, there are a couple of things you can try.

If you judge that the complaint is justified, and you want to placate the enquirer and reassure them that you will put things right, try smiling. It can subtly change the character of your voice and perhaps ease the situation. This doesn't mean a grin suggesting that you're not taking the complaint seriously, or a rictus implying that you're scared stiff; just do what common sense would suggest you do if the complainer were standing in front of you and you may well find that you can defuse the situation as a result.

If you feel you're being browbeaten with an unjustified complaint, or if you think the complaint is justified but the enquirer is overreacting or even bullying, that can be pretty intimidating. You may relapse into confusion, tempting the complainer to press home their advantage, or you may lose your cool, with potentially disastrous consequences for your customer relations. So you could try continuing the conversation standing up. Your enquirer can't see that you've stood up so can't regard it as provocative, but it can give you the extra confidence you need to regain the situation. Of course it may look odd to those around you but that doesn't matter; it's the person at the other end of the phone you have to be concerned with.

Now a quick health warning: these techniques don't work for everybody. So just try them if you feel inclined and see if they work for you. One thing you must do, though, is take phone complaints more seriously than you would complaints delivered in person. You've no idea how long the person at the other end has had to get worked up, and you can't use your facial expression or body language to show that you're empathizing. Remember – people who think they've had bad service tend to tell three times as many people as those who've had good service, and they really embellish the story. Mistakes sometimes get made, but it's how you rectify them that matters.

Responding to text-based messages

Just as you should never take an oral enquiry at face value (whether face-to-face or by phone) so you should treat enquiries by e-mail, text, messaging or web form with caution too. Just because the act of composing an e-mail gives the enquirer the opportunity to state their requirements succinctly and comprehensively, that doesn't mean that they'll actually do so. (Remember the 'diver' versus 'driver' incident above.) So the all-important supplementary question that we looked at in Chapter 1 is no less crucial here.

Responding to a text-based message with a supplementary question has another benefit too: it reassures the enquirer that you've received their enquiry and are working on it. Because it's not an instantly interactive medium, sending an e-mail or text is an act of faith for the enquirer. They've no idea that it hasn't just gone into a void until you respond.

And you don't necessarily have to respond using the same medium either.

If you've received an enquiry by text or e-mail, a quick phone call may be a more efficient way of obtaining the further information you need, and can also demonstrate to the enquirer that you're treating their request with urgency. But if you do decide to respond to an e-mail with an e-mail, you need to be ready for perhaps several further e-mail exchanges before you can 'close the deal' on the work to be done.

It's better if this exchange can happen fairly rapidly, so it may be worth delaying your initial e-mail response until you know you have the time to handle several back-and-forth communications in rapid succession. There's no guarantee that it will work out like that of course – your enquirer may have gone into a meeting or lecture immediately after sending their enquiry – but it's wise to be able to make yourself available in case they do respond quickly.

Enquiries received by text should be prime candidates for a response using a different medium. As we saw in Chapter 1, the apparently briefest and simplest of requests can conceal a great deal more detail that requires investigation by you, and the cramped and tiny screen of even the most generously proportioned phone is probably not the best display device to use. So perhaps you could text back a quick holding response and ask if you can either talk directly or (if there's time) get some further background by e-mail.

Then there's the issue of how you respond to messages that are full of contractions (e.g. 'cul8r') and rounded off with a smiley face. Do you reciprocate, risking misunderstandings if your own contractions aren't self-evident? Or do you keep it formal, with the danger that the enquirer will dismiss you as stuffy and devalue the help you might have been able to offer as a result? No answers to such dilemmas yet, but we will return to them when we look at how you can present your answer well, in Chapter 6.

The same principle applies the other way around too. If you receive an enquiry by phone, an e-mail response outlining what you've agreed to do can both reassure the enquirer and provide the start of an audit trail. This could be highly desirable if you have to hand the enquiry on to a colleague, which is something that we'll be looking at in the next section.

Keeping good records

We touched on record keeping in Chapter 1. We looked at how your note taking during the initial dialogue with the enquirer should enable you to confirm exactly what you intend to do to help them, with no misunderstandings, providing neither too little information nor too much. We've also seen how important it is to agree an unambiguous deadline for the work.

Record keeping matters at all times, not just to enable you to keep track of the progress of enquiries but also to provide longer-term evidence of the value of the service you provide. However, it's probably true to say that when you have your enquirer physically with you, you're less likely to lose track of them or forget what you were doing for them, so the need for a really detailed record of the enquiry may not be quite so crucial. But when your enquirer isn't there at all, then a good record becomes absolutely essential.

As we've already seen in this chapter, you can't keep going back to your remote enquirer to ask supplementary questions. Each time you do so they'll assume you're going to provide the answer, so they'll be understandably peeved if it's just another question about something you forgot. You'll also need at least two methods of communicating with them – phone and e-mail, for example – because if you don't you can be sure that the moment you need to contact them urgently their phone will be out of range or their laptop battery will be flat.

So it really helps to use an enquiry record form that covers everything you might need to ask. What kind of form? That's for you or your management to decide, and we'll come back to some enquiry management packages that you could use in Chapter 8. But there are some other things we need to consider first.

Privacy

You're almost certainly going to record personal information about your enquirer – name, contact details, what they want and why. So your organization needs to be registered for data protection, detailing the specific purpose for which you need to record and hold the information that you use to identify the enquirer. The details may vary from jurisdiction to jurisdiction, but your organization is likely to be required to guarantee (among other things) that it will only use the information for the purpose for which it has been collected, that it will not collect any more information than is necessary, and that it will keep it for no longer than it needs to.

This can raise some tricky issues. How much is enough information for the purpose, when you may have had to delve into the enquirer's motives for asking to ensure that you can provide an answer appropriate to their needs?

What does keeping the record only for as long as necessary mean? Just till the initial enquiry is completed? The enquirer may want to come back later asking you to take the investigation further – and may be relying on you to have kept a record of what you've done so far. And you'll certainly want to use the results of completed enquiries to add to your performance data and perhaps for your own know-how or Frequently Asked Question (FAQ) files.

Whatever way you (or your management) has resolved these issues, you may need to reassure the enquirer that you are permitted to record personal data for enquiry answering purposes, and that you will (of course) treat their request in confidence.

Audit trail and ownership

Whatever information you decide to record about your searching, you'll need to ensure that you have enough detail to enable you to report back to the enquirer on how you tackled the task and what progress you made. When the enquirer isn't actually with you, it's not necessarily so easy to keep checking back with them as and when you find things, so you need a good research record to present to them at the end if necessary. Equally crucially, you may need to hand the enquiry over to a colleague, so you have to make sure that your colleague doesn't waste time by going over sources and search strategies that you've tried already.

And at every stage in its life, someone needs to 'own' the enquiry. When you first take it, and agree the task with the enquirer, that someone is you. It's perfectly all right to transfer that ownership to someone else – someone taking over from your shift, for example, or a subject specialist better qualified to answer – but the buck always has to stop with someone and that someone needs to be on the record.

What to record . . .

Every information service's needs are different, so the decision on exactly what to record has to be yours (or your manager's). But here's a checklist of items to consider:

The enquirer
- name
- organization

- address
- postcode (worth recording this in a separate field in case you ever want to do market research based on your enquirers' location)
- phone number
- mobile number
- e-mail address
- fax (unlikely these days – but you never know)
- special contact instructions, such as 'try mobile first, e-mail second'; 'call between specific times'; 'don't mention subject of enquiry to whoever picks up the phone.'
  (Try to get at least two contact points in case the preferred one isn't working when you need to report back and the deadline is looming. If you're taking enquiries using a web form, make sure that the contact information goes into a 'compulsory' field, which the enquirer has to fill in before the enquiry will be accepted.)

The enquiry
- narrative description (as much detail as necessary)
- deadline (date and – if necessary – time)
- enquiry taken by . . .
- enquiry transferred to . . . (there could be several of these).

Enquiry analysis
- Who? What? When? Where? Why? How? (As discussed in Chapter 1.)
- What will the final answer look like? (More on this in Chapter 3.)
- Focus, dynamism, complexity, viability (More on this in Chapter 3.)
- Who really needs to know this? (As explained in Chapter 5.)

Search strategy
- root terms, broader terms, narrower terms, related terms (More on these in Chapter 4.)
- sources tried (The list of Starter Sources in Chapter 8 may help you here.)
- search results (What you found – and where.)
- the answer. (We'll deal with how you might present it to the enquirer in Chapter 6.)

Sign-off
- who completed the enquiry

- who delivered the answer (may not be the same person)
- degree of success in answering it: complete; partial; compromise
- how satisfied the enquirer was (not necessarily the same as how successful you were)
- if the enquiry was referred to someone else, then who?
- how long it took to answer (hours and minutes)
- when completed (date and time)
- delivered on time? If not, why not?
- follow-up actions (e.g. add new information to FAQs, know-how files or Starter Sources – there's more on sign-off activities in Chapter 6).

This may seem like an awful lot to record. But if answering information enquiries on behalf of your users – in a public reference library or as a researcher working for an organization – is part of your job, it's difficult to see how you can avoid going through each of these stages. There may be a case for recording less if you're working in a university, college or school library, where it's the students who are supposed to be doing the research and not you. But even here, demonstrating good research practice can be a crucial part of your learning support role and keeping a record of what you've advised can both help future students and demonstrate to the authorities the value of the contribution the library makes.

Whatever your view on this, the enquirer and enquiry details are essential, and you'd be recording these during the initial dialogue anyway. The same probably goes for the Who? What? When? Where? Why? How?

The other elements of the enquiry analysis are pretty essential too if you're actually doing the research on the enquirer's behalf, as we'll discover in later chapters, and you'll need to record them as you go along. It's only sensible to record the stages in your search strategy, to ensure you don't accidentally go over the same ground twice – and it's essential to do so if you have to hand a half-finished enquiry to someone else. And as for the sign-off details – well, they provide crucial performance data that you may depend on when bidding for next year's funding (or even staving off cuts) and they can also help you deliver a more efficient, customer-focused service next time. All in all, then, there isn't much you can really afford to leave out.

. . . and how to record it

Well, you could always use the tried and tested paper enquiry form – but this does seem to be missing an awful lot of tricks. You're dependent on an increasingly dog-eared piece of paper that could get mislaid at any stage in the process – especially if you transfer the enquiry to someone else. Your audit trail is compromised. And, crucially, gathering performance data from a stack of paper forms is an incredibly labour-intensive operation.

There are plenty of packages available that enable you to keep track of progress on enquiries. Some need to be adapted from other applications – IT helpdesk job tracking, for example – but there are also some packages specifically designed for library and information enquiry work. Or if you wanted to, you could try creating a form tailor-made for you, using standard database or spreadsheet packages.

There's a list of software packages and services that may be suitable for keeping track of enquiries – whether face-to-face or remote – in Chapter 8.

Coming next – avoiding panic, thinking on your feet . . .

Now at last you have all the information you need to actually start hunting for the answer. But where are you going to look? This is often the time when your mind goes blank and you start to panic. But there are techniques you can use to help you see your way from mystery to potential solution, and deal with your panic at the same time. So in Chapter 3, we'll look at how to get started on answering your enquiry.

To recap . . .

- **With remote enquiries, you're deprived of most of the clues we take for granted when dealing with people face-to-face.**
- **The risk of misunderstanding – even of offence – is high.**
- **Use good customer service techniques to keep your enquirer on side.**
- **Good record keeping is essential when your enquirer is somewhere else.**

CHAPTER 3

Getting started

Dealing with panic – thinking clearly

In this chapter you'll find out how to:

■ **imagine what the final answer will look like**
■ **decide what kinds of source will provide that answer**
■ **determine the best delivery medium to use**
■ **start identifying actual sources.**

Fear of the unknown is the strongest kind, the horror fiction writer H. P. Lovecraft is supposed to have said. Well 'fear' may be pitching it a bit strong in this context, but if you're anything like most people at this stage in the enquiry answering process, you're certainly feeling pretty nervous and possibly starting to panic. You've listened carefully to your enquirer. You've asked sensible questions. You know exactly what they want. Now your enquirer is waiting for you to help. And you haven't a clue where to start looking.

Fortunately, there are techniques for dealing with this. All you need is a little bit of thinking time. You can buy this time with a positive response – something like: 'I'm sure I can help; let me just think for a moment where the best place to start would be.' You'll pick your own form of words, of course, but having a response like this ready all the time is going to be really useful. Firstly, it dispenses instant reassurance to the enquirer; you've promised to help. So, secondly, that means the enquirer will metaphorically step back and give you the few seconds' thinking time you need. Thirdly, of course, a response like this commits you to nothing. It certainly doesn't commit you to finding the answer, because you don't know whether you can do that yet. But it does commit you to helping – and you can always help.

Imagining the final answer

To deal with the 'fear' – or at least the panic – you need to turn the unknown into the known as quickly as possible: in this case, knowing where to go to find the information the enquirer needs. You've just bought some thinking time to help you do this, so how are you going to make the best use of it? It's tempting to simply look busy – turn confidently to the nearest printed reference source you can find, or click onto a search engine and pretend you know what you're doing. Resist the temptation! You're wasting both your and the enquirer's time with this pantomime, you're not getting yourself any nearer to a solution, and the enquirer will quite likely realize that you're just playing for time.

No – you can actually do something much more useful with this thinking time: employ a fundamental technique of enquiry answering that you probably need to deploy with every enquiry you ever tackle. Remember we said in Chapter 1 that even if you rarely asked a hypothetical question of the enquirer, there was one hypothetical question that you almost always had to ask yourself? Well this is where it comes in – and the question is:

What is the final answer going to look like?

If you could magically see the answer in your mind's eye, on the page or on a screen, what would be in it and how would it be laid out? You can't yet see the fine detail – the actual words of the answer, for instance – and you certainly don't know yet whether there is a source that will provide an answer that looks like that. But you do at least now know what you're aiming for and that will allow you to narrow down the options for where to look. Just as there was a posh phrase for the structured conversation we discussed in Chapter 1 – the reference interview – there's one for this process too: predictive search. Use the phrase if you like – but all it really means is starting to turn the unknown into the known, and that's a great way of helping you deal with the panic.

Just think of some of the forms the final answer could take . . .

Text is the lifeblood of any information and library service and it comes in many forms. It could be long, as in a book or report; short, as in an article or news item; or variable, as in a less formal document such as a blog posting. In each of these cases, the text would be continuous, telling a coherent story from the beginning to the end of the document (or more usually in the case of a blog, from the end to the beginning). But text can also be broken – designed to be read in little chunks – as in an encyclopaedia, dictionary, directory or series of blog comments. And it isn't necessarily printed; it can take the form of original manuscript records as well.

Tables of figures are scarcely less important. So much of human knowledge depends on counting and measuring that the answer you need will frequently include information presented numerically. This needn't necessarily be static; the figures may be presented electronically, allowing them to be instantly updated whenever any of the data changes. And the rapidly growing practice of mashing data to produce new datasets just means that figures will continue to grow in importance.

Graphs or charts are just another way of presenting those figures that are so fundamental to human knowledge. They may lack the precision of the figures on which they're based, but they may be much more effective at demonstrating what the figures mean.

Lists are another bedrock of human knowledge and they come in many forms: checklists, directory entries, bibliographies, search results and new resources created by mashing lists together.

Pictures have grown hugely in importance for enquiry answering since the time that crisp images and video on the web replaced muzzy photocopies from books. Like text, they come in many forms. With fine art, contemplation of the picture is sufficient in itself; illustrations usually support text; with news pictures or video, capturing the incident and publishing it quickly matters far more than technical quality; and then there are unimaginable quantities of self-published personal pictures and video clips.

Diagrams are just a stylized form of picture designed to express something graphically. They can be technical, medical, managerial and much more. They can be animated as well as static and, like the figures and graphs, they can be updated in real time.

Maps are a further form of picture or diagram and can illustrate just about anything. Geo-spatial information is also fundamental to human knowledge, so we use maps to show topography, geology or climate, illustrate trends, show economic, social or scientific information graphically, and follow routes.

Sound recordings can take the form of radio broadcasts, webinars, podcasts or momentary 'sound objects' like a sound effect or jingle. They can be delivered in a continuous stream in real time or packaged for replaying whenever required. Like pictures, sound now plays an infinitely more important part in answering enquiries as the web has developed.

You'll probably be able to think of many other forms the final answer could take now you've got the idea – but try not to think yet in terms of printed documents, electronic or online content. That comes a bit later. Just think about what the final answer would look like, irrespective of the medium through which it's delivered.

While you're doing your thinking…

When you have the enquirer with you, they can see that you're going through a systematic procedure and they'll probably be happy to wait while you carry out your preliminary investigations. There's no great problem if you're using a text-based medium to deal with the enquiry either; you can sign off, do your thinking and get back to them as soon as you have something to report.

But on the phone, it's different. Silences can seem achingly long to the person at the other end, so it's a good idea to let the enquirer know what you're doing while you investigate – not necessarily a continuous running commentary but certainly a series of regular short bulletins explaining what you're finding and what you intend to do next. It may well be that the enquirer can also contribute ideas while this is going on, so it can in effect be a continuation of the structured conversation with which the process started. But be slightly cautious if the enquirer starts suggesting actual sources to try at this stage; they may have very good ideas of course – but remember that advising on possible solutions is your job, so don't risk being misled by a well-meant but ultimately ill-informed suggestion.

Of course you could put the enquirer on hold, leaving them to listen to an endless loop of music that isn't to their taste. But if you do that the enquirer has no idea what's going on – doesn't even necessarily know if you're still there – and their impatience may start to rise again. So if you think your preliminary investigations may take a little time, perhaps suggest that you'll call them back. Guarantee when you'll do that – and make sure you either meet or beat that deadline.

We'll have a look at how imagining what the final answer will look like – or predictive search if you will – works out in practice in a minute. But before we do that, there are some other important decisions you need to take first: what are the best kinds of source and delivery medium to use, and do you have the resources to tackle the enquiry at all?

Choosing the best type of source and delivery medium

Make no mistake – the internet is a vital tool of enquiry work, and the web is the best single enquiry answering tool we have. Screen-based media offer enormous advantages over print in allowing you to search rapidly through unimaginable quantities of content and providing instant access to your chosen information source. But the fact is that print on a page is still a uniquely valuable medium, and we should be very cautious about predicting its demise, because forecasts like that almost invariably come to grief.

Now, these days that doesn't necessarily mean ink on paper. E-books are rapidly becoming a widely accepted alternative and screen technology is improving all the time, making the content more and more comfortable to read and the experience increasingly close to that of reading ink on paper. Studies also suggest that reading content on a tablet computer may be a much pleasanter experience than on a laptop – although that's for you and your enquirer to judge at the time.

However, there's also evidence to suggest that people who read traditional print on paper may actually retain more of what they read in memory, and may also need to read less of the document to understand its main themes than they might have to do if they were reading it on screen. Screen-based media still don't match the flexibility you can achieve by spreading open publications out on a desk, marking their pages, arranging them in piles. By all means browse online for information and ideas; but when it comes to serious reading, print – or at least a very good electronic substitute for it – is a far more comfortable medium to use.

So as well as deciding what your enquirer's requested information will look like, you also have to determine certain of its other characteristics. Only then can you decide on the kind of source that may be best suited to the purpose, and the best medium to use in delivering it. It's likely to be a crucial decision for the way you present the answer to your enquirer, and it's something you should have been able to determine from some of the Why? and How? questions you asked earlier. The characteristics of the subject that you need to consider at this stage are . . .

Focus, dynamism, complexity, viability
Focus

Is the information required broad-based and comprehensive or narrow and specific?

We've already seen the dangers that can arise when an enquirer says 'Get me everything you've got on...' It's very unlikely that they literally mean 'everything'. But sometimes people really do want a broad overview of a subject. They might be gathering background information as a preliminary to a more detailed study, or they may just want to brief themselves for a meeting, interview or short-term project. So here are some suggestions for types of source you could try. Don't worry too much about the delivery medium just yet – print or e-book, web page or Portable Document Format (PDF) document – we'll come onto that later. Some of the ideas here may suggest print on paper to you – but try not to make that assumption yet.

For broad-based, comprehensive information, you could use:

- an entry in a general encyclopaedia
- a chapter in a textbook
- a complete textbook.

But if your enquirer has got beyond that stage, and is delving into a subject for more narrow and specific detail, you could try:

- an entry in a special encyclopaedia
- an index entry in a textbook
- a report from a specialist organization (i.e. not a conventional publisher)
- a journal article or news item
- a statistical table
- an entry in a directory
- a database record
- a website or page.

Dynamism

Is the information required static or dynamic?

Static information is complete – finished. It's a matter of history. That's not to say that new research won't be done into it in the future but, to qualify as static, the subject must have reached a full stop at the time your enquirer asks you about it. Deciding whether information is static is a hazardous undertaking. Stonehenge may be thousands of years old, but if the enquirer is looking for information on new archaeological finds that tell us more about its purpose or method of construction, that means that the information required may not be static at all. Your When? or What? questions (trying to find out what aspect of Stonehenge the enquirer is interested in) should have helped you to establish that.

But, assuming that you are certain that the information you are being asked about really *is* static, print on the page (whether ink on paper or a high-quality e-reader) is going to be a perfectly acceptable way of satisfying it, and may offer a more comfortable reading experience than looking at, say, web pages with all their extraneous and off-putting surrounding content.

Dynamic information is changing now; a developing news story is a classic example of dynamic information. So you need to be sure that you've opted for a delivery medium that allows the enquirer to keep up with events. Nevertheless, there are degrees of dynamism; a weekly source – whether a printed journal or its online equivalent – may well be sufficient for keeping up to date with medical research, papers for which are frequently submitted months before publication. Stock market prices, on the other hand, can change second by second and require at least a near to real time service to keep up with them.

So bearing in mind these variations in dynamism, you'll need to opt for a medium that will enable your enquirer to keep up with events as they happen. That's likely to mean a continuously or regularly updated medium such as a web page or a feed (tracking updates to information on a particular site). These may not represent as comfortable a read as a printed book or e-reader page, but the need for the information to be as up to date as possible trumps the need for reading comfort.

One thing you may find yourself having to do with dynamic information is browsing and scanning through the content you find. Because the information is fast-changing, it may only have been indexed automatically, with no allowance for any of the synonymous, broader or narrower terms that you or the enquirer may have used (although growing use of semantic technology, taking account of the meaning of the words and the context in which they appear, will increasingly render this less of a problem). So you might have no alternative but to read quickly through quite a lot of text – a selection of news stories, perhaps, or a lengthy article. We'll look at strategic reading techniques to help you do this in Chapter 4.

Complexity

Is the information about a single concept, or is it multifaceted (concerned with how two or more concepts relate to one another)?

Single concept enquiries can almost always be summed up in a word or a short phrase – 'dogs' or 'town planning'. That doesn't necessarily mean, however, that information on them is going to be easy to find; you might be looking for rare occurrences of a single word or phrase buried in a mass of text. Nevertheless, to answer single concept enquiries you might be able to find a book or an article (whether ink on paper, print in an e-book, a PDF document or a single website) using nothing more complex than your own library catalogue or discovery system or an all-purpose search engine.

Multifaceted enquiries, on the other hand, are concerned with the impact of one concept upon another – something like 'the health risks of rabies spreading from wolves in central Europe to domestic dogs' or 'the town planning law implications of non-retail uses of shops in conservation areas'. To find acceptable answers to questions such as these you'll need to make more sophisticated use of search engines – using the power search option or Boolean logic, for example (more on these in Chapter 4). But you'll do even better if you identify a specialist database to search in the first place – a health database in the first instance, perhaps, or an environmental one in the second. (We'll consider how to identify specific sources shortly.)

Finally, a word of warning: the focus, dynamism and complexity of any subject can all vary according to your perception of it. We've already seen that an enquiry's dynamism can be measured in minutes or years – and your perception of an enquiry's focus and complexity may well depend on the environment in which you work. If you work in an academic library that supports courses in statistics or demographics, then you'll probably regard the Welsh migration query as pretty general and none too complex either, whereas someone in an all-purpose reference library, or working for a specialist organization that normally has no need for demographic information at all, might see it as very specific and complex indeed. Which leads us on neatly to…

Viability

Do you have the resources to answer this enquiry in-house, and is the answer likely to be found in a published source?

The first of these two problems is likely to be the easier to deal with. If you provide an information service that specializes in science, you probably won't have much in-house on the arts. You have access to all the resources of the free web of course – but so does your enquirer, so they're looking to you for more than that. They may expect you to be able to source documents on unfamiliar topics for them, or at the very least to advise on specialist institutions or sources that they could access or visit. A library in a law firm may be primarily concerned with law – but the litigation in which the firm is engaged at any one time may be concerned with any subject under the sun, and the lawyer will be expecting you to provide them with the background information they need to fight the case.

When it comes to whether the information your enquirer needs is in any published source at all, you're on much shakier ground. It's actually very difficult to say with any certainty that information isn't published anywhere. Even the most comprehensive of search engines, for example, covers only a fraction of the content on the web – not to mention all the older documents that haven't been digitized yet and information from the many developing nations that still aren't well represented in mainstream resource guides or retrieval tools. And you can also be sure that, as soon as you tell your enquirer that the information they need isn't published, they'll find it themselves by serendipity. So this might be an occasion when you need to seek out not documents but expert help. But who to ask? We'll return to what to do when you can't find the answer in Chapter 5.

Print, electronic documents, online

The whole point about taking time to determine a subject's focus, dynamism and complexity is to help you decide which delivery medium would be most appropriate for the job. So before we try this out on some real enquiries, let's review the advantages and disadvantages of each.

Printed sources are easy to handle, user-friendly, carry no running costs and don't need electricity to make them work. You don't need to explain to an enquirer how to use a printed source, and print on paper is a very comfortable way of taking in information – so you can hand a printed source over with the minimum of initial help. But printed sources can also be out of date, slow to use if you are hunting for information buried in the text, and inflexible if their indexing doesn't accommodate the approach the enquirer wants to take. So they're only really good for static information.

Electronic documents means fixed content stored in a digital format. This used to be something like a publication or database on a CD-ROM, but now it's much more likely to be an e-book read on a special reader or a journal delivered to a tablet computer – and we also need to include PDF documents in this category too. As with the printed sources, the content they contain is fixed – once the document is published, that's it until the next edition – and they have the further disadvantage, compared with printed sources, that they need to be charged up before you can use them. However, unlike printed sources, they may enable you to search for information buried in the text reasonably quickly – albeit with varying degrees of sophistication. So they can be quite good for finding more focused information.

Online services (delivered via a browser or an application on a tablet computer or smartphone) can be right up to date, and the range of opportunities they offer for finding the one piece of information you need quickly are legion. But you do have to satisfy yourself that you can trust what you find, and you can be swamped with poor-quality information in the process. Often you'll need to take a decision on whether to go for a professionally edited specialist online service instead of just relying on the free web. If you do, you may find greater accuracy and searching flexibility – but you either have to pay for all the content you download or else need to ensure that the terms of your licence allow you to provide the information to your enquirer. But with these caveats, online services should be good for information that is dynamic and multifaceted.

Does all this really work?

Let's see how all this would work with just some of the questions that our different types of enquirer posed in Chapter 1. We'll start with a particularly straightforward one, to illustrate how the principle works and show just how precisely you can define the final answer using this technique. It's the one that started with a request for books on retailing.

What is Marks & Spencer's current pre-tax profit?

What will the final answer look like?	This is about as straightforward an answer to visualize as there can be – it's going to take the form of a single monetary figure, attached to a company name which you already know, with a very recent date.
Focus	Narrow and specific; the enquirer wants just one figure.
Dynamism	Could be very dynamic; the announcement might only have come this morning, or the last quarterly result might have been a couple of months ago – which begs the question: when is the next one due?
Complexity	Single concept; there's been no mention of the figure being put alongside other results – for example, to produce accounting ratios – which could have turned it into a multifaceted enquiry.
Viability	It's a very common request, so it should be available in plenty of published sources, several of which will be accessible anywhere.

Likely type of source and delivery medium	The figure will certainly appear somewhere on paper, but because this is a business topic and timeliness is important, you're more likely to find it on a screen. All but the smallest of companies these days have a corporate website, so that's the obvious first place to look. Larger companies, like Marks & Spencer, also publish glossy annual reports, so that's an alternative.
	Failing that, you could try something that gives information on a lot of companies – such as a company directory or database. You could perhaps try the business pages of a newspaper to look for news of the company's latest results – but since you'd be looking for one specific piece of information buried among thousands of others, it would be far more sensible to use a searchable news website.
	But of all these possibilities, one source trumps all the rest: the company's own website. It's easy to find, will be guaranteed to have the most up-to-date figure, and – because company announcements are regulated by legislation and, in this case, by stock exchange rules too – you can trust the answer.

Get the idea? Now let's look at a few of the other enquiries below.

I'm looking for information on migration patterns in Wales.

What will the final answer look like?	This is a request for information that will track and measure the movements of people. If it's about measurement then it will have to take the form of figures presented as statistics. However, there could be textual commentary on the figures, and they could also be presented as a graph, chart or diagrammatic map.
Focus	Depends what sources you have access to; it's pretty broad-based if you have plenty of statistical and demographic sources to hand and can offer the enquirer lots of options, but it's narrow and specific if you don't, because the enquirer wants one type of population data only.
Dynamism	Relatively static at the moment; censuses tend to be taken only once every ten years, albeit with more frequent intermediate population estimates. However, this is likely to change as more and more countries move on to rolling census-taking.
Complexity	Fairly multifaceted; although this is a standard census enquiry, it does involve combinations and permutations of figures about people and places.
Viability	Since plenty of government information is now published online, finding the basic data should present few problems. After that, though, it will depend on whether the data is available in a form that is useful to the enquirer, and how much additional information, such as commentary on the figures, they want.
Likely type of source and delivery medium	You're looking for statistics on the movement of people. Such comprehensive data could only be gathered by some sort of government agency like a national statistical office, which is likely to publish the information both in statistical serials and (because more and more government data is available online) on the web as well.
	But censuses aren't necessarily taken that frequently so the latest available data could be a few years old; so is there any way of updating it with interim estimates?
	Also, the enquirer may want to be able to manipulate the figures to mash the data into new datasets – in which case they're going to need it in spreadsheet form.
	Finally, if the enquirer also wants commentary on these migration patterns, or maps and diagrams, they might be worth looking for in sociology or demographic textbooks – or possibly in a journal produced by the census-taking authority.

I'm doing a project on the Westminster Aquarium.

What will the final answer look like?	We're looking for information on a Victorian building in London – not a first-rank one either, like the Crystal Palace (which our muddled enquirer mentioned). There'll be descriptive text and pictures but, because it's not a particularly important building, you're probably not going to find very much about it in any one place.
Focus	Narrow and specific in that you're looking for information on just one building – but that may have to change if the enquiry turns out not to be viable.
Dynamism	Static; initial exploratory searching will reveal that this Victorian building was pulled down years ago, and was never of the first rank anyway. So pretty much anything you find, no matter how old, will probably be useful.
Complexity	Single concept; with an obscure topic like this, you can't afford to be choosy.
Viability	Hard to say. There will surely be some basic information available on the web, if only because virtually any topic, no matter how obscure, attracts its own enthusiasts. Whether you can find enough material on that narrow and specific topic to satisfy the requirements of the enquirer's assignment remains to be seen.
Likely type of source and delivery medium	Detailed textbooks on Victorian architecture or specialist guides to London's historic buildings may yield something, but because it's a relatively obscure building you're probably going to have to hunt through quite a lot of printed indexes to find anything at all. Perhaps the enquirer's idea of the *Illustrated London News* is worth following up – if the printed version has a decent index or if the archive has been digitized. As we've already surmised under 'viability', the building might even have 'friends' – enthusiasts who might share information about it on the web – but if you followed this up you'd need to be sure that the information they provided was reliable.

Cash for Parliamentary questions … Strong & Moral Britain Association … neo-fascist organizations … funding … school governors … declarations of interest.

What will the final answer look like?	Quite a shopping list of different kinds of information here. If the cash-for-questions affair is a hot topic in current affairs right now, then this could take the form of fast-moving news. For the association, you need not only neutral directory-type information about its activities but also (because it's dubious) something probing and investigative – which might suggest a news source again. The school governor information is going to take the form of rules, regulations, codes of practice – that sort of thing.
Focus	Broad-based and comprehensive? Not really; it's actually three narrow and specific enquiries, all linked in the enquirer's story.
Dynamism	Depends on which aspect you're investigating. The cash-for-questions affair could have flared up recently or might have been dormant for years.

Ditto the stuff about the association; you'll certainly want the most up-to-date information you can get about its whereabouts, activities, governance and funding but don't know yet whether the neo-fascist issue is current or long past.

It will be important to have the current version of the school governor rules, but we don't know at the moment how frequently they change. |

Complexity	Multifaceted throughout. The 'cash for questions' concept will need to be linked to the name of the MP brother, and subsequently to the 'Strong & Moral Britain Association' and 'neo-fascism' concepts.
	The rules for school governors are likely to be more straightforward because they'll be packaged somewhere – in a handbook or on a website. But it would still be helpful to home in quickly on the specific issue of declarations of interest, so this part is multifaceted too.
Viability	You'd think information in the cash-for-questions affair and the Strong & Moral Britain Association would be readily available on the web. But the enquirer is keen to hush all this up, so if it is that easy to find it why have they come to you? This part of the enquiry could be much less viable than it might at first appear.
	The school governor rules should present few viability problems. Lots of people are school governors, they'll all need the rules and guidelines, so these are likely to be pretty accessible.
Likely type of source and delivery medium	There's a lot here, so let's take the sources stage by stage.
	An online news source should deal with the cash-for-questions affair – provided you can find an archive that goes back far enough. Or if there's too much you could try filtering the amount of information you have to deal with by searching through the political weeklies instead. However, 'cash for questions' isn't the only phrase that could be used to describe the affair, so you'll probably need to think of other search terms to use and adapt the search in the light of new information discovered. (We'll come back to the principles behind this in Chapter 4.)
	Basic information on the association might come from a directory or the association's own website, but comment on its more dubious activities is more likely to have appeared as investigative journalism in newspaper features, journal articles or whistle-blowing blogs. Fortunately you do at least have a precise name to search on – but then won't the enquirer have done that already?
	Finally, if it's not obvious from a web search where the official version of the rules for school governors can be found, think about the kind of organization that would publish them – the relevant government department, local education authorities, associations of school governors – and look for those organizations instead.

Identifying actual sources

So now at last we've reached the really hard part – trying to discover whether any actual sources exist that provide your ideal solution. This is the really daunting bit (isn't it?) – having to learn hundreds of sources and have their details always at your fingertips, so that you can be ready at all times to come out with an instant diagnosis that always seems so impressive when doctors do it. It's true – there are an awful lot of information sources available, and you can spend an entire career answering enquiries and still be discovering new ones on your very last day at work.

But reassurance is at hand. First of all, successful enquiry work depends on constant daily practice, so the more you do it, the easier it becomes because you can remember more sources without ever having consciously learned them. (Actually this can be a danger as much as an advantage; if you get too used to going to one particular source, you tend to continue using it even if a newer more efficient one becomes available.)

The other reassurance, though, is that you can function perfectly effectively by keeping just a few multi-purpose reference sources in mind. Take a look at the list of Starter Sources that feature in Chapter 8. Between them, they will get you started on a very high proportion of the enquiries you will encounter. As the title of the list implies, they are only a start, and many information professionals would dispute some of the choices and want to substitute alternative candidates of their own. Nevertheless, what these sources (or others like them) can do is set you on the track of other, more specialized sources that you can't possibly be expected to remember.

Learning some basic ones

So the basic principle is: get to know a limited number of the most useful sources that you have immediately to hand – whether physically in the library or available virtually through your discovery system – plus a selection of really useful web-based resources that you know you can rely on. There's no great mystery to this. If you're working in a public reference or college library, it will already be well stocked with sources of this kind, and you can spend some time profitably in the early stages of your new job browsing through some of them to see what they can do for you. Two tips. First, if you're operating from a traditional enquiry desk, concentrate to begin with on the sources shelved immediately behind you. They will be the ones that your more experienced colleagues have found the most useful over the years. And, secondly, when you are examining and evaluating an unfamiliar source, don't just flick or scroll through it at random, but make it do something for you. If it's a directory or a statistical journal, look up a specific organization or figure. If it's a printed source, follow up all the index references to a subject of your choice. If it's electronic, give it a really complex task to perform and see how quickly it responds and how relevant its answers are.

It would also be worth exploring any kind of know-how file that your colleagues may have compiled. It's likely to represent the fruit of years of accumulated collective experience of enquiry answering and (if you'll forgive the mixed metaphor) can be a gold mine of hard-to-find information, once tracked down and never forgotten. It could be a database on your intranet, a set of bookmarked favourite websites accessible centrally somewhere, an FAQs kind of offering or a wiki-type application to which colleagues can add whenever something strikes them as useful. Whatever form it takes, it will be well worth getting to know in detail, because it will be uniquely tailored to your own organization's information specialities and the kinds of questions your enquirers are in the habit of asking. (We'll return to resources of this kind in Chapter 6 when we look at signing off the enquiry.)

But what if you're operating on your own, with sole responsibility for the library or information service of a specialist organization and no one to turn to for help? Well, you could try going through the list of Starter Sources in Chapter 8, visiting each website in turn where there is one, and seeing whether any of the featured sources might be of use to you. Most of them are professionally edited charged-for services, so the links will just take you to a description of the source from which you can make your judgement as to its value to you. But some of the Starter Sources are free, so you can obviously use those straight away. And if you want to see any of these resources in printed form, you could try awarding yourself an afternoon off, going to your nearest large public reference library or to your university, armed with the Starter Sources list, and ask to see as many of them as you can. Then use them to find out which journals, directories, statistical serials, websites and databases might help you in your work. (We'll look at how to get started in a new job of this kind in Chapter 7.)

Coming next – smarter searching...

Now that we have a pretty good idea which sources we're going to use, and the most efficient delivery media for the purpose, we can actually get down to looking things up. This can present plenty of pitfalls, which we as professionals need to learn to anticipate and avoid. So in Chapter 4, we'll think about strategies for systematic and efficient searching.

To recap . . .

- Remember that there are techniques you can learn for stopping your mind from going blank – without having to know any actual sources.
- Begin by visualizing the final answer in your mind's eye – a long or short piece of continuous text, a list, table, diagram, picture, map, multimedia recording.
- Decide on the focus, dynamism, complexity and viability of the enquiry – that will help you determine the best kinds of sources and delivery media for the job.
- Finally, start looking for specific sources, bearing in mind that you will only ever have to learn a small number of multi-purpose reference sources in order to begin tackling most enquiries.

CHAPTER 4

Smarter searching

Tips for efficient search strategies

In this chapter you'll find out how to:

■ search systematically
■ avoid traps for the unwary
■ make the most of searching tools
■ read strategically
■ decide whether you can rely on what you find.

There's a saying in show business that amateurs rehearse until everything goes right and professionals rehearse until nothing goes wrong. It's a great definition of the difference between an amateur and a professional, in any profession.

Just think how it works with a show. Amateurs haven't a clue what could go wrong, so they have to rehearse everything equally. Professionals have the training, the knowledge, the experience to know where the danger points in a production are – the rapid scene change, the complex piece of business – and concentrate on those. Yet amateurs can manage to put on a good show eventually, with practice. And exactly the same applies to one of the most hazardous parts of enquiry work: searching.

The problem is that, since everyone has access now to an apparently limitless pool of instantly available information, anyone can assume that they're an expert searcher. So information professionals – the ones who earn their living by searching, or advising people on how to search – have to be able to demonstrate that there are ways of searching smarter, even when they're using exactly the same tools as their enquirers.

Who needs to be able to search smarter?

The short answer is: everyone. It doesn't matter whether you're doing the searching yourself or helping others to do so, you need to understand the principles behind it so that the whole process happens as smoothly and efficiently as possible. Just think why . . .

If you're working in a **public reference library** you may well find yourself dealing with people to whom searching doesn't come naturally. A personal visitor may require a lot of hand-holding while you help them discover the information they need. At the same time, a queue may be building up at the enquiry desk – or, if you've gone on an expedition to the shelves with your enquirer, other people may start hovering round waiting for you to become free. So however you decide to help, you have to make sure that your search strategy will work, quickly. If the enquiry has come in by phone, and you've agreed to do some preliminary searching on the enquirer's behalf – seeking out some likely references, for example – then you'll have agreed a deadline with them (won't you?) and you'll need to be sure that you can meet it, even if you encounter complications along the way.

It may be a bit different in a **school**, **college** or **university library**. Of course you're not going to research the student's assignment for them; that's their job. But you have a vital role nevertheless in ensuring that they learn good searching habits from the outset – not bad ones. So you're likely to be suggesting search strategies they can adopt when they come to you seeking help – and when their search doesn't work for any reason, it's you they'll be turning to for advice on why it hasn't and what they can do to remedy the situation. And if they phone or text in for advice, or e-mail you, you may find yourself at the very least having to do trial searches yourself before you can help them. Information literacy – knowing how to find information and whether you can trust it when you do – is a fundamental life skill now, and it is part of your job to nurture that skill in students.

If you're a researcher in a **specialist organization** then you may well be responsible for the entire process – from taking the initial enquiry to delivering the finished answer, with a hefty amount of desk research to do along the way. Obviously in these circumstances, your smarter searching skills are paramount. Your enquirer probably won't be interested in how you arrived at the answer, but they will want to be satisfied that the answer you've provided is accurate, complete and reliable. Remember, too, that your enquirer may actually be pursuing their own (perhaps less efficient) researches in parallel to yours. It can be very embarrassing if they turn up serendipitously something that you've failed to find when supposedly searching systematically.

Just as in any other profession, there's a wealth of specialized technical and theoretical learning behind searching, which grows more and more multi-layered the more sophisticated the available tools become. But when you do it every day, the fundamental principles of smarter searching needn't be rocket science; at its most basic, it's a question of anticipating where the pitfalls lie and making sure they don't happen – and a lot of that simply comes with practice. So some tips on smarter searching…

Working out your search strategy

Because we began by imagining what the final answer would look like, and worked out the likely delivery media by determining the enquiry's focus, dynamism and complexity, we already have a list of potential sources that we could try. So it's obviously wisest to go to the one that's likely to give the best results first. Why? Because if we do find the answer there we can stop looking, secure in the knowledge that the other sources on our list would have been less fit for purpose. And what do we mean by 'fit for purpose'? That means deciding whether we need:

- the most **up-to-date** source
- the one most **relevant** to the subject
- the one most **appropriate** to the task in hand.

Let's see how this might work with some of the enquiries we've been dealing with.

I'm looking for information on migration patterns in Wales.
Numerical census data is the core to all this. It wins on two of the three counts: it's **relevant** (all about population and their movements) and **appropriate** (you're looking for figures, at least to begin with). It may also be as **up to date** as you're going to get, even though full censuses tend to be taken only every ten years. However, you may also have to consider where to look for later estimates of population movements since the last census; they should be more **up to date** but will probably be less detailed. And since the enquirer is trying to identify migration patterns, then informed commentary on the

trends – in textbooks or journal articles – would also be both **relevant** and **appropriate** to the approach the enquirer wants to take.

I'm trying to find a song called 'When I Would Sing Under the Ocean' *[but the title is probably wrong]*.
Go for the most **relevant** source first – an encyclopaedia or dictionary (whether print or electronic) or reliable website that lists song titles. It doesn't necessarily have to be particularly **up to date**, since you've already established that it's a more traditional song, not one that's likely to be currently in the charts – unless your enquirer wants to buy a recording, that is, in which case some kind of **up-to-date** resource (such as an online record store) will be essential. Of course, all the evidence so far suggests that the title is wrong and that no amount of looking up, in print or electronic sources, is going to unearth it. So it may turn out that asking a musical expert is the most **appropriate** course of action.

Cash for Parliamentary questions ... Strong & Moral Britain Association ... neo-fascist organizations ... funding ... school governors ... declarations of interest.
This is actually more than one enquiry, so we need to consider each of its elements separately.

The cash-for-questions affair may or may not be a developing story now. So it's best to assume initially that it is and go for the most **up-to-date** source first, such as an online news service.

For the Association a professionally edited archive database of documents dealing with current affairs or social issues seems the most **appropriate** starting point, since you will need to test speculations about funding and links with neo-fascist organizations.

For the guidance for school governors, the school itself (or its local education authority) might seem the most **relevant** place to go, but it's hardly **appropriate** since your enquirer doesn't want to alert the school. So generic information on school governors' duties and obligations, from the government department responsible for education, or from some kind of umbrella body for school governors, should be equally **relevant**, and – bearing in mind the enquirer's need for secrecy – far more **appropriate**.

Searching systematically

Now you've decided how you're going to set about your searching, what are you going to search for? Plenty of things can go wrong – things that we as professionals ought to be able to avoid – so among the myriad things that can cause problems, here are some that you should certainly consider.

Variant spellings

It doesn't matter whether you're using a printed index or a search engine, variant spellings can cause big problems. So try to anticipate them. Proper names are especially tricky; it was Cain who killed Abel in the bible story, but Citizen Kane who had a sledge called Rosebud in the eponymous movie. And where on earth do you start looking for the fast-food chain that calls itself *Mc*Donalds but dubs its culinary pièce de résistance a Big *Mac*? Many of the best reference resources – whether print or electronic – are American, so you will have to watch out for 'color' instead of 'colour', 'disk' instead of 'disc', 'skeptical' instead of 'sceptical'. This may not be a great problem with printed indexes; your eye will quickly spot the difference. Large scale search engines, too, may help you with a 'Did you mean…?' prompt. But you can't necessarily rely on this feature being available on simpler search engines embedded within individual websites – so if you search for 'favourite' or 'labour', on an American website it may keep on giving you a zero result no matter how much you swear at it. There are plenty of other pitfalls with variant spellings in British English too – jails can be gaols, choirs can be quires (in more archaic sources anyway) – one could go on but that's enough.

Homonyms

If you're looking for do-it-yourself supplies and keep coming up with foodstuffs instead, you've hit the homonym problem associated with 'nuts', which is equally at home in the two phrases 'nuts and bolts' and 'monkey nuts'. Scholars studying the indented wax symbols at the base of legal documents run the risk that their hunt for 'seals' will lead them to sea mammals. And specialists in literacy keep finding themselves being vexingly directed to a large Berkshire town when they look up 'reading'. You need to be particularly alive to the dangers of homonyms, and be ready with tactics for taking evasive action if necessary. It's particularly – but not exclusively – a problem with free-text searching – i.e. when you're not able to take advantage of any controlled vocabulary feature such as an online taxonomy. You can reduce the risks associated with homonyms by adding a further qualifying term to your search – such as 'manuscripts' for 'seals' or 'literacy' for 'reading'. But this technique just raises further complications if you try to qualify 'nuts' with a term like 'hardware', because your qualifying term also has two definitions: DIY materials or computing equipment. So in this case, using a trade classification code (if it's possible to search on those in the source you're using) instead of the word will probably be a better option. In fact, whenever you're searching electronically, do keep an eye out for any links that look as if they might lead to an onboard thesaurus or other authority file of preferred terms that can help with your searching precision.

British versus American terminology

We've already seen some of the problems that American spellings can throw up, and of course it's exactly the same with American terminology – words that are different in British and American English. We all watch Hollywood movies (or do we mean films?), so most people would probably remember to use 'elevator' instead of 'lift', 'streetcar' or 'trolley' instead of 'tram', and 'pants' instead of 'trousers' (although this last one presents its own special homonym problems as well; 'pants' can also mean short, fast breaths, or be a slang term for 'useless' or 'bad'). And when it comes to more technical terminology, how many Europeans know that the American for 'central heating' is 'space heating', and is probably equally difficult to find whether you are using a printed index or a search engine? Finally, too, remember that dates are cited differently in America and Europe. As all the world now knows following the tragic events at the World Trade Center, 9/11 is 11 September in America – but in most of the rest of the world 9/11 would mean 9 November. So if you're using a search engine that permits date searching, make sure you have the elements in the right order.

Making the most of indexes

Really well-constructed indexes are based on a thesaurus that allows for all the different approaches that a searcher could take towards a subject. Alas, however, the real world is full of ineptly constructed indexes. An 'amateur' index, maybe compiled by the book's author, might be full of elementary mistakes that a professional indexer would avoid. Such indexes might include an entry for 'railways', for example, but fail to add a parallel one or a reference for 'train services'. A professional indexer – a member of the Society of Indexers, for example – would avoid such mistakes; but a professional indexer will probably be on a fixed fee based on the estimated time taken to complete the job, so may not have the time to index down to the level of detail that would be helpful to you. And don't think it's necessarily going to be any better if you're using a search engine; that's only going to be as good as the algorithm that drives it and the words and phrases that are available for it to index. So it's wise to assume that, whatever kind of index you encounter, whether presented as a printed alphabetical list or searchable using some kind of electronic retrieval tool, it will have its limitations and there will come a point where you will have to fend for yourself.

Synonymous, broader, narrower and related terms

When you were discussing the task with your enquirer, you or the enquirer are likely to have jotted down a list of possible words and phrases to search under. That's fine as far as it goes, but with only a little extra effort, you can create a far more valuable searching aid for yourself. So instead of just jotting down those words and phrases randomly, in the order they occur to you, try listing them in a structured way. What you'll be doing is creating your own mini taxonomy – specially designed to help you with your current enquiry. It will minimize your chances of missing something relevant and – just as important – it will help you to avoid wasting your time by accidentally going over the same ground twice. And exactly the same principle applies if you're helping a student with a project, or a member of the public to become self-sufficient with their searching. By introducing them to techniques such as these you'll be helping them improve their information literacy and empowering them as well.

Let's see how it might work in practice. Suppose you're researching – or helping someone research – information on reptiles of the Galapagos Islands. As your enquirer has been explaining their needs in response to your questioning, you should have been jotting down possible search terms – words and phrases to search under. (If you've been left on your own to do the research on someone else's behalf, you can think of possible search terms by discussing the subject with a colleague and, again, noting down likely words and phrases as you talk together – or you can even discuss the subject with yourself if there's no-one else to help.) Anyway, whatever you do, this is the list you've ended up with:

> **reptiles**
> **Galapagos Islands**
> **animals**
> **islands**
> **Pacific Ocean**
> **tortoises**
> **iguanas**
> **volcanic terrain**
> **fauna**
> **tropical islands**

Not a bad start, but it only takes another minute to turn this into a far more valuable searching aid. What you need to do first is to separate these words and phrases according to the different concepts they represent. There are clearly two concepts here, the animals and the place, and – guess what? – we're back with the Who? What? When? Where? Why? How? that we used when originally discussing the enquirer's needs. So here are all those terms again, but rearranged this time according to the concepts they represent:

Who?	Where?
reptiles	Galapagos Islands
animals	islands
tortoises	Pacific Ocean
iguanas	volcanic terrain
fauna	tropical islands

The last stage in the process of making all your terms fit for use in searching is to rearrange them one more time, into a natural hierarchy. This time, we'll just focus on the Who? concept. The enquiry is about 'reptiles', remember – so 'reptiles' is your **root term**. Then looking down the list again you can see a couple of **broader terms** – the generic word 'animals' and the more scientific one 'fauna'. Finally, you have some **narrower terms** – words that fit within the category of 'animals' or 'fauna' and also within the 'reptiles' category; these terms are 'tortoises' and 'iguanas'. So what you end up with is a mini-taxonomy:

Broader terms	animals, fauna
Root term	reptiles
Narrower terms	tortoises, iguanas

Now if you're inclined to think that this is all a rather tedious process to have to go through, just bear three things in mind. First, this is a deliberately simple example to demonstrate the principles clearly; you'll frequently find yourself dealing with much more complex concepts than this, encompassing many more possible terms to juggle with. Second, if you're not doing the research yourself, but helping a student or a member of the public to do it, your use of this technique can both help them to work more efficiently – and hence finish the job quicker – and also demonstrate to them that you are a professional who knows where the pitfalls lie and how to avoid them. And third, we'll discover in a moment how this process really pays dividends when you start applying it to the indexes you use in your researches – again, whether you're dealing with a printed alphabetical index or terms retrieved by a search engine. So let's start to see just how useful it can be.

Printed indexes

It's when things start to go wrong that your careful preparation for searching will really pay off. Hunting for information is a journey into the unknown. Every source you use will be differently constructed, and have its own indexing quirks. As your searching progresses, you're bound to come across relevant words and phrases that you never thought of in the first place. If you do, your mini-taxonomy should at least help to ensure that you don't merely repeat work you've already done. Let's go back to those reptiles; suppose you've looked through a few sources, and you suddenly find the following entry:

iguanas *see* land iguanas, marine iguanas

A 'see' reference should mean that the indexer has decided to put no index entries under the term you used, and is redirecting you instead to (in this case) two different places where you should find all the relevant index entries for each kind of iguana. Alphabetically they're widely separated, so you'd never have found them in a printed index if the indexer hadn't given you this essential guidance. So the first thing you need to do is amend your mini-taxonomy like this:

Broader terms	animals, fauna
Root term	reptiles
Narrower terms	tortoises, iguanas
Subset of narrower term	land iguanas, marine iguanas

The second thing is to decide whether or not to go back over previous sources and recheck them for the new terms. This is where your systematic approach again pays dividends, because if you do decide to go back to previous sources, you can do so secure in the knowledge that you only have to check under the newly discovered terms, since you can guarantee that you've already searched systematically under the terms you thought of in the first place. If there's nothing extra to be found under the new terms, then you should be able to abandon the source without wasting any more time on it. (We'll discuss efficient management of your time in Chapter 5.) Anyway, back to your printed index searching and the next thing you come across is:

reptiles *see also* predators

This is the indexer trying to be helpful. Since many reptiles are predators, they've judged that anyone looking for reptiles might either be interested in broadening their search out to include predators in general or, alternatively, may be interested only in the predatory habits of reptiles – not their habitats, mating rituals or whatever. With a 'see also' reference, you should expect to find entries in both places in your printed index – the place where you originally looked and the additional place that you've been directed to – because the two terms are not the same and don't appear in the same place in the taxonomy that you've created. In this context, 'predator' is a **related term**. It doesn't fit in your mini-taxonomy at all, because – unlike reptiles such as snakes or crocodiles – tortoises and iguanas are exclusively herbivores. But it's far better to be alerted to the possibility of further terms to search under than not, and that's the function of 'see also' references in printed indexes.

Electronic searching aids

Electronic media can offer a whole range of additional searching aids, with a speed and accuracy that you usually can't match using a printed index. Such tools include search engines – whether a large-scale generic search engine or a search window on a specific website – and other finding tools of the kind that you might encounter on a PDF reader or a browser. We need to consider the two types separately.

Search engines can, for example, save you the bother of thinking of all the forms in which your search term could appear by automatically looking for other words with the same root as the one you've used. If you're doing a search on surface transport, for instance, and put in the term 'rail', the search engine could come back with references to 'railway' and 'railroad' – but might also retrieve documents on 'railings', so you have to be constantly on your guard. Increasingly, too, search engines will try to anticipate what you're looking for, coming up with possible words or phrases even before you've finished typing, and thereby perhaps alerting you to better terms to search on as a result. Some can even accommodate natural language searching, attempting to process a complete sentence or phrase for its sense and returning an immediate, finished answer. And if you've mistyped something, a search engine might well suggest a correct spelling.

But the problem is that – unlike a printed index, which you can potentially review in its entirety – you can't easily determine the way a search engine does its indexing. Search engines crawl websites (or, in the case of an embedded search engine, one specific website) looking for terms to index, and then an algorithm interrogates the index, trying to match your search to the indexed terms. But there are two problems here: first, the process is invisible to you and, second, an algorithm is only a formula, applying logic to the task but without any knowledge of the reason or motive for the interrogation.

Searching software will probably attempt to return results ranked for relevance – but that simply means that the algorithm automatically tries to determine the importance of a document to your search according to things like how frequently your search term appears in it, whether it's in the title or on the home page or in the metatags (information provided on a website to help search engines categorize it correctly), or how frequently the document is linked to from others. All these might help to narrow the field, but no matter how sophisticated its construction, no algorithm can replicate the rich complexity of thought going on in your head as you assess each document retrieved and constantly relate it in your mind to what the enquirer actually needs. A search engine can frequently give you a good start, but that's probably it.

Other finding tools have even more limitations. A PDF reader will let you search for any word or phrase in the document you're reading, and can offer extra help by displaying the retrieved terms in the context in which they appear, so you can decide which might be the best occurrence of the term to look at first. It can also find different forms of a word – if you type in 'employ', it should also retrieve 'employed', 'employer', 'employment', 'employs' and so on. But it will only find additions to the exact character string you enter, and can't suggest possible alternatives with different spellings. So if you enter 'employment' and the concept always appears in the document as the word 'job', you won't find what you need even though the concept of employment may have been there all the time. The same applies to the tool supplied with browsers that lets you find words or phrases buried in the web page you're looking at. You have to think of all the synonymous, broader, narrower and related terms for yourself – and that comes back to your mini-taxonomy.

Advanced search capabilities, which many search engines offer, can really help you exploit your mini-taxonomy to good effect. Whether you're using a large-scale generic search engine or one embedded within a single site, take a look around in the vicinity of the search window to see if there's a link to an advanced search or 'power' search option. You can make good use of it if you're doing a complex, multifaceted search with many different terms to describe each concept. Advanced search interfaces come in many different forms. They can be presented as a simple matrix that will allow you to be as flexible in your searching as you need. Or they may be more prescriptive, giving you pre-set options for – for example – retrieving only documents in which all of a given set of terms appear, or documents that contain any one or more of a selection of words, or specifying that you want to search for a specific phrase. Depending on the site, the advanced search feature can sometimes also allow you to limit your search by date and place (the When? and Where? concepts).

Boolean logic is what drives advanced searching and it's really helpful for any searcher to be able to understand how it works because it can be a very powerful retrieval tool indeed. It works by linking words or phrases together using the logical operators OR, AND and NOT. You can frequently use Boolean logic directly in a basic search engine window, typing in not only the search terms you want to use but also the logical operators that show how you want the terms to relate to one another. However, the symbols and syntax that you need to use for your Boolean searching can vary from one search engine to another, so we're just going to look at the principle here.

A search on:	Retrieves:	The result is:
tortoises OR iguanas	all the documents on tortoises, all the documents on iguanas and (therefore) all the documents that mention them both together as well.	you get high **recall** (a lot of documents retrieved) but not necessarily high **relevance** because this search retrieves absolutely everything, including documents that contain only passing references to either species.
tortoises AND iguanas	only the documents that mention both tortoises and iguanas.	you get lower **recall** (because you retrieve none of the documents that mention only tortoises or only iguanas) but quite possibly higher **relevance** because the smaller number of documents retrieved might focus specifically on tortoises and iguanas together.
tortoises NOT iguanas	documents that mention tortoises, but not when they also mention iguanas.	you get somewhat lower **recall** (because you've excluded all the iguana documents), but you may have compromised your **relevance** too, because you've also excluded some potentially relevant tortoise documents – the ones that also mentioned iguanas.

But this is just the start. You could, for example, construct a search that says: 'I want all the documents on tortoises or iguanas of the Galapagos Islands, except for marine iguanas, which I want to exclude.' In straightforward Boolean logic (ignoring the specific symbols and syntax that any given search engine might use), that would look like this:

((tortoises OR iguanas) AND "galapagos islands") NOT marine

Searching efficiently, making the most of all the tools and techniques available, is a significant skill in its own right. So if you want to be really effective at it, it's worth reading up on the subject constantly and going on regular training courses to keep up to date with the latest innovations.

Reading strategically

Sometimes, none of the searching tools at your disposal work. You may find yourself dealing with a printed document whose title and contents page suggest that it's going to be relevant, but it doesn't have an index in which you can look up the precise topic you're interested in. Or you may have retrieved a lengthy PDF document or densely packed web page, but the simple word search tools you have at your disposal just aren't coming up with the results to confirm your suspicion that it's likely to be useful because you clearly aren't using the same terminology as the author has chosen. In these circumstances, rather than ignoring a potentially useful source, you may have no option but to skim through the actual text, looking for the nuggets of relevant information that you're pretty sure must be in there. It may sound daunting, but there are ways of tackling this. The trick is knowing which words you can safely ignore.

Now we haven't lost sight here of the possibility that you might not be doing the searching yourself but supporting a student or member of the public in their researches. Hopefully, by now you've already demonstrated your professionalism in helping them avoid the searching traps that many amateurs might fall into. So now's your opportunity to empower your enquirer even more by introducing them to some basic strategic reading techniques. Here are the main ones that you can try:

- Look at the document's signposting first – title, subtitle, standfirst, executive summary, conclusions or findings or recommendations, section headings, bullet points, lists, boxes, captions. Between them, they can help you or your enquirer navigate your way through the document and hence locate the parts where the information you need is most likely to be found. (Be slightly wary of executive summaries, though. Although they might appear to give you everything you need, their job is to draw the reader's attention to what the author thinks is important. An executive summary may ignore supporting information that doesn't necessarily advance the document's main argument, although it's exactly what you or your enquirer are looking for.)

Then, if you do have to sample the complete text:

- Read down the middle of the page, relying on your peripheral vision to spot significant words. Try not to swivel your head; if you do that, persistence of vision will kick in and everything will blur.
- Alternatively, if you're faced with long lines of print, you can bounce your eye from the left half to the right half of the page, stopping and sampling the text each time.

What are you looking for? Well, perhaps for significant words and phrases that will indicate you're on the right track. Once again, your trusty mini-taxonomy should tell you what those words and phrases are, including synonymous, broader, narrower and related ones. However, the problem with this is that, if they're all in lower case, those words and phrases won't look any different to the eye from all the other text around them. So look in addition for the following elements, which will be easy to spot because they stand out from the rest of the text and also offer the best clues as to the document's content:

- **Capitalized words**. These are the names of people, organizations, places – possibly even concepts. They're the sorts of words that will indicate if you're on the right track.
- **Abbreviations**. These are shortened forms of the names of those organizations – or possibly concepts. So they offer similar clues to those offered by the capitalized words.
- **Numerals**. As we saw in Chapter 3, counting and measuring forms the basis of a great deal of human knowledge, so numerals of any kind – numbers, percentages, dates, monetary values – can also give you valuable clues as to the document's relevance to your enquiry. When you spot a numeral, pause, cast your eye to left and right seeing what's being measured, and decide whether it's relevant.
- **Words in non-standard typography**. Text in bold, italic or small capitals is also easy to spot and may offer valuable clues. Be slightly wary of these, though. Unlike abbreviations and capitalized words, the decision to emphasize something using non-standard typography is a subjective one made by the author, so may reflect what the author believes is important, not necessarily what you're looking for.

And finally – a first-rate technique for getting through longer documents really quickly:

- **Read the first sentence of each paragraph**. If the paragraphs are reasonably long – say more than three sentences – it's astonishing how easy it is to follow a document's main argument by just reading the first sentence. Of course, this technique doesn't work when the paragraphs are just a couple of sentences each – you have to read so much of the document that you're unlikely to save yourself much time. But when the paragraphs are longer, you can get through an enormous amount of text extraordinarily quickly.

You may think of all this as 'rapid reading'. It isn't really, of course. You're just reading at your normal reading speed. The trick is knowing what not to read, and it only works if you already have a pretty clear idea of what you're looking for. Your eye won't instinctively spot a significant word or phrase unless you've already worked out what those words or phrases are – so constructing your own mini-taxonomy is just as important for browsing and scanning as it is for using indexes. And one final tip: if the text you have to read is on a screen, print it out first – or at least print out the executive summary if you think you can rely on it. The screen flickers, the lights flicker, and the resolution is probably clearer in print anyway. So give your eyes a break by making it as easy as possible for them to spot what you're looking for.

Making sure that what you find is reliable

Years ago you used to be able to work on the principle that, if you saw a piece of information in three different places, it was probably true. Then along came the web – the ultimate vanity publishing medium. Now anyone can publish anything, regardless of whether or not they know what they're talking about, and an error on one website can be replicated over and over again on others. So before we leave the issue of smarter searching, we need to think about whether you can believe what you find.

Once again, this is a crucial lesson to get home if you're helping someone else with their researches too. Part of information literacy is being able to evaluate what you find – and if you're supporting students, for example, an essential part of your role as a responsible information professional is to encourage the habit of evaluation whenever you can. So what practical steps can you take?

Quality-controlled sources

First, start with professionally edited, quality-controlled sources if you possibly can. Rather than just using a search engine straight away, begin by looking up likely sources for the information you need in a directory, bibliography or source guide – the kinds of resources you can see in the list of Starter Sources in Chapter 8. Sources like these have some measure of editorial control exercised over them, so they're much safer to use than just calling up a search screen on the web and hoping for the best. Obviously they don't restrict themselves to resources on the free web; they'll include references to authoritative printed and electronic documents, and to charged-for services delivered online. But probably the commonest type of information they provide is web links so, using such sources, you can get to useful places on the web just as quickly as you might when using a search engine – but with far more confidence that you can trust what you find.

And when you do start exploring likely places on the web, try following links from the sites that you are recommended to use to other relevant sites. If you've satisfied yourself that the site you're using is reliable, then the sites that it links to are pretty certain to be reliable as well, so this is an altogether safer way of exploring resources on the web than simply going back to a set of search engine results and trying the next one on the list in the hope that it will be better. Beware, though: the web is full of tempting byways. So make sure you keep track of where you've visited, and also that you're still really addressing the enquirer's needs. It's all too easy to get sidetracked.

Who's saying it and what's their agenda?

Once you think you're on to something that might provide the answer, you need to screen it for two things: **authoritativeness** and **agenda**. If you're using a printed source or electronic document, look round the preliminary material – introduction, preface, blurb, 'about the author' – to determine how qualified the author is to merit your trust. And if you're looking online, try the site's 'about us' page. So what are you looking for? It basically comes down to two things: authoritativeness and agenda.

Authoritativeness: If it's an individual that you're assessing, what are their professional and academic qualifications, how has their career developed, are they currently working in an appropriate field and at an appropriate level of seniority or responsibility? If it's an organization, what kind is it (government, regulatory, research, professional, trade, charity, society, club), how long has it been established and what are its significant achievements?

Agenda: It's probably safe to say that there's no such thing as value-free information. All information is provided for a purpose, and the mere fact of presenting some information means that other information must have been suppressed. So again, you need to satisfy yourself that you understand where the author of the information is coming from. If it's an individual, what are the values or philosophies that they espouse? If it's an organization, what are its aims and objectives, and who funds it?

If, for example, you read that alternative energy is inherently more cost-effective long term than nuclear power, you need to know whether an academic research team, an energy industry organization or an environmental pressure group, is saying it. If you're doing the research on somebody else's behalf, providing information on the authoritativeness and agenda of the source you've used isn't an optional extra, it's an essential part of the answer. If you're supporting a student in their researches, then inculcating in them the habit of always determining a source's authority and agenda is one of the best services you can render.

Trust no one!

So is there any kind of source that you can trust implicitly? Probably not. Even the most reliable reference sources go out of date, so at the very least you need to decide whether what you're using matches the dynamism of the enquiry. Printed sources may have been through a slightly more formal publishing process than electronic ones, but there's still no substitute for finding the evidence that proves they can be relied upon. In any case, there's such a huge crossover between printed and electronic delivery now that the distinction between media no longer makes any sense in this context; the same document may well come out as a printed report, a PDF that can be read on a computer, tablet or e-reader and an HTML file designed for a browser. In addition, electronic documents can be created by anyone at little or no cost – so it's worth concluding by considering four specific types.

Blogs (short for 'weblogs') are online diaries that anyone can create and post on the web, using simple software. Their numbers are growing at an extraordinary rate and, by their very nature, they are completely uncontrolled. Some of the main search engines enable you to search blogs specifically. You can find blogs on the most esoteric of subjects, offering not only information but also the possibility of putting your enquirer in touch with a blogger who may be able to help them directly with their query. Obviously if you recognize a blogger as an acknowledged specialist in their field – contributing a regular column to a trade or professional journal, for example – then you can presumably trust the blog. If you don't, then once again you need to assess the blogger's credentials, and probably double check the blog's information elsewhere as well.

Microblogs are a subset of the genre. For technical reasons, these can't exceed 140 characters in length, so the information they contain is very compressed. They're also very quick and easy to write and publish, so they can represent off-the-cuff remarks that haven't necessarily been well considered. All the caveats that relate to blogs apply to microblogs too – but probably more so.

Wikis use special software to allow groups of people to contribute collaboratively to the same body of content and then edit or amend it. Wiki applications can appear on the web, where anyone could use them, or on a single organization's intranet, where they're only accessible to a closed group. Typical web applications include communal encyclopaedias, or services that allow whistle-blowers to publish leaked documents anonymously. Conventional wisdom might suggest that wikis are inherently untrustworthy because anyone can amend them irrespective of their qualification to do so. However, they also tend to be self-correcting, as errors or omissions may be quickly spotted by others and amended accordingly.

Open access is a movement among academics, researchers and professionals to make the full texts of their refereed articles and papers freely and permanently available online to anyone who wants to use them. There are two complementary forms of open access publishing. Either authors can provide access to their own published articles, by making their electronic copies available free for all. Or journal publishers can provide free access to the articles – either by charging the author or institution for refereeing and publishing them (instead of charging the user for accessing them), or simply by making their online edition free for all. As the open access movement grows, it should result in more and more high-quality peer-reviewed content, whose reliability you can trust, being made available on the web.

Coming next – even more things that can go wrong...

Smarter searching can help you stop a lot of things from going wrong and, as we've seen, can enable you to empower students or other library users whose researches you're guiding. But this isn't the only time when things can go awry. So in Chapter 5, we'll think about what to do when you're running out of time and still no nearer to finding an answer.

To recap . . .

■ Enquirers have access to many of the same searching tools as you do – your job is to help them search smarter.
■ Consider whether you need to use the most up-to-date, the most relevant or the most appropriate source before you start.
■ Remember the pitfalls posed by variant spellings, homonyms and British versus American terminology.
■ Where a search is likely to be complex or lengthy, construct your own mini-taxonomy before you start – and remember that all indexes, whether printed or electronic, have their limitations.
■ Learn and practise strategic reading techniques, for when there's no index.
■ Make sure that you can trust whatever you find.

CHAPTER 5

Help! Everything's going wrong

When you can't find the answer and you're running out of time

In this chapter you'll find out how to:

- **prioritize enquiries so the right ones get done first**
- **think of compromise solutions when time's running out**
- **decide what to do when you can't find the answer**
- **look for outside help.**

Would-be library censors have challenged John Steinbeck's novel *Of Mice and Men* more than almost any other book, according to the American Library Association. Of rather more importance to us at this stage in the enquiry process, though, is the line by Robert Burns from which the book's title is taken: 'The best laid schemes of mice and men gang aft agley.' If you've stayed with us thus far, you'll have established precisely what the enquirer wants, without any ambiguities, worked out logically where the answer can be found, and searched systematically and professionally for the information you need. But you still can't find it, and time's running out.

It would be all too easy to feel the panic returning at a time like this. Enquirers really do think that the web has it all and you can get at it instantly, and that can trap you into agreeing to an unrealistic deadline, despite your efforts to avoid it. So what you need to do is to manage their expectations while making sure you can deliver what you've promised – which is why it's so important to settle the matter of the deadline from the outset (as we discussed in Chapter 1).

But is the deadline always your problem? It clearly is if your job is to find information on behalf of other people. But what about when it's a student who's come to you with a really complex assignment which (as they so often seem to do) they've started far too late. Well, to be hard-nosed about it, you have two choices. You can tell them it's their problem and they should have thought of it sooner, leaving them to go off disgruntled with you and the library – or possibly to waste the time of a colleague on another desk in a different department. Or you can demonstrate your professionalism in advising them what they can do in the limited time available, thereby casting yourself in the role of mentor rather than critic.

So let's start by going back to some of the basics of time management. You should find them useful in helping you organize your own work – whether enquiry-related or otherwise – and if you're able to instil them in the students or members of the public you help, then you'll be conferring a benefit on them too.

Vital versus urgent tasks

We discovered in Chapter 1 that 'urgent' is not an acceptable deadline for any enquiry. You need to know how urgent; you need a date and/or a time. Now we need to take that a stage further and make sure that we really understand what we mean by urgency. Faced with a limited amount of time and a number of competing tasks, you need first of all to sort them into priority order and allocate time between them – and you need to revise that timetable constantly as new tasks come along to demand your attention. To do this, you need to be clear about how urgent each task that lies before you is – but, just as important, you also need to decide how vital it is to your organization.

Just as there are posh terms for your initial structured conversation with the enquirer (the 'reference interview' – in Chapter 1 – remember?) and for imagining what the final answer will look like ('predictive search', in Chapter 3), so there's a posh term for this process too: triage. Usually applied to health care, it's the process of prioritizing patients to ensure the ones with the severest conditions get treated first when resources are limited but that no one gets neglected altogether. But it's also used to prioritize business decisions, and problem solving in IT – and it's certainly applicable to enquiry handling.

So let's think of the distinction between these two terms. A **vital** task is one without which your organization can't function. An **urgent** task is one that has an imminent deadline; it may or may not be vital. Yet we often tend to be panicked by the idea of something being urgent without always considering the bigger question of how vital it is.

If you don't buy information sources, install, catalogue and index them, learn how they work and keep up payments on the subscription, then you can't answer the enquiries. So these are vital tasks. But they're not necessarily urgent; if you put them off until later, no great harm may be done. They may in due course become urgent. If you're constantly being asked for information that's sitting in a document that you haven't yet catalogued, or a piece of software that you haven't yet installed, or is only available through a service where the subscription has lapsed, then fixing the problem becomes not only vital but also urgent. So it follows from this that the sensible way to prioritize your work is:

1 vital and urgent
2 vital but not yet urgent
3 urgent but not particularly vital
4 neither vital nor urgent.

Now you might argue with the relative priority of items 2 and 3 and may want to reverse their order depending on the specific circumstances – but you get the principle. Now let's see how it might apply to enquiry work.

First come first served?

Let's say that you're a researcher with three urgent enquiries to do. They all have the same deadline. But one is for a colleague doing a college course on day release, another is for your boss and the third is for a client of your organization. Your job is to answer enquiries for all these three people, so they're all vital; if you don't do them, you'll be in trouble. But if you fail your colleague you'll probably just get ticked off; if you fail the boss you might lose your job; and if you fail the client, everyone might lose their jobs. So you can see that there are degrees of urgency, depending on how vital the task is. You might deal with this challenge by:

1 suggesting an appropriate source for the colleague to use for him or herself
2 warning the boss that you're doing an enquiry for a client and either providing a brief holding answer for the boss or negotiating a longer deadline (or both)
3 concentrating on the client.

Once you've prioritized your competing enquiries in the manner outlined above, you can then work out how long you need to allocate to each. Five minutes with your catalogue or a couple of other finding aids may be enough for your college colleague, and 15 minutes looking up, downloading and e-mailing over a few pieces of information will put the boss on the back burner for a while. This leaves you the rest of the morning to spend doing database searches, scanning journal references and compiling a list of results for the client. (And preparing to present the answer in a helpful way; we'll look at adding value in Chapter 6.)

Of course, it doesn't work like this in a busy public reference or college library. There every enquirer is equally important, and you have to employ different techniques to ensure that everyone's deadlines are met. To do this, you really need to be able to assess instantly the relative difficulty of answering each enquiry, and the amount of time you'll need to devote to it. There's probably no easy way of doing this; it comes with experience and, even then, you'll still encounter some enquiries that turn out to be almost impossible to answer, even though you thought they were going to be easy. But you can help yourself by making sure that you do know your basic reference sources really well – just a strictly limited number of them, such as some of the Starter Sources listed in Chapter 8. If you are familiar with their contents, then you should know what's feasible and where you're going to have to negotiate with the enquirer about providing a compromise answer.

Time is money

Difficulty doesn't necessarily equate to time (although it might). An alternative to spending time on a difficult enquiry might be to use a charged-for database, where the time saved justifies the expense. Assuming that you've correctly identified the right one to use, fully searchable databases can save you an enormous amount of time – not least because they fail as quickly as they succeed. Just think about it for a moment. If you use printed sources, it takes you longer to fail to find the answer than it does to succeed because, once you've found it, you stop looking. Whereas if you keep not finding it, you go on looking until you've exhausted every possibility. A database search, on the other hand, fails as quickly as it succeeds by telling you instantly that there's nothing available on your chosen subject – so you know much further ahead of the deadline that an enquiry is going to be difficult, and you still have time to do something about it.

The moral here is that time is money. Whether you choose to spend money on a charged-for search that takes five minutes, or restrict yourself to available printed sources or the free web and spend an hour searching that way instead, the result is the same – cost to your organization. In making efficient use of your time, and deciding when to call a halt and compromise on the answer instead, you must always bear in mind that every minute you spend on an enquiry is costing your organization money. It's not just the cost of your modest salary either, or the download or copying charges; there are overheads to take into account as well – things like lighting, heating, rent and local taxes, to say nothing of the cost of acquiring and managing all your information sources in the first place. The less efficiently you plan your search strategy, the more it costs your organization.

Your working timetable

We've already done some assessment of the relative difficulty of some of our sample enquiries, in Chapter 3 – by imagining what the final answer would look like, deciding what kinds of source would provide an answer that looked like that and determining the enquiry's viability in terms of the resources at our disposal. Assuming that they all have the same deadline (and that you do have access to all the sources necessary for answering them), let's go back to the seven enquiries we started with in Chapter 1, assess them for how easy or hard they're likely to be, and whether they're likely to be quick or slow to complete.

Then we'll use these assessments to sort the enquiries into priority order, so that everybody gets started as quickly as possible. This means that you deal with the easiest and quickest enquiries first, rather than keeping people with simple enquiries waiting unnecessarily while you spend time on the slower and harder ones. On that basis, the order of priority for tackling these enquiries may come out looking like the following table.

Priority	Enquiry	Assessment	Verdict
1	What is Marks & Spencer's current pre-tax profit?	Just a little bit of thought (or discussion with colleagues) should have suggested plenty of possible places to look, including simply going straight to the company's own website.	Very **easy** and – once you've worked out where to go – extremely **quick**.

(continued on next page)

Priority	Enquiry	Assessment	Verdict
2	I'm looking for information on who's doing research into the health risks of artificial and natural radiation (and it's worth searching elsewhere if we don't find the article the enquirer thinks they remember from *New Scientist*).	Your enquirer didn't help to start with by just asking for one source when what they probably needed was a fairly extensive literature search. However, there are plenty of sources that provide references to scientific literature – albeit frequently charged-for services – although it may take a little time to find suitable articles from them.	Pretty **easy** in that there's no shortage of easily identifiable resources giving access to scientific literature, so reasonably **quick** to get started, at least. But if the enquirer really wants comprehensive information on who's doing what, hunting enough material out to satisfy them could prove a bit **slow** in the long run.
3	I'm looking for information on migration patterns in Wales.	A very small quantity of looking up – on the national statistical website or in a printed statistical digest – should start to provide the raw numeric data you need. But your enquirer may be looking for commentary on and explanation of the patterns as well. That information could be much more widely dispersed among books, reports, journal articles, blogs – although there are still plenty of source guides you could use to locate it.	Fairly **easy** in that there are plenty of possible places to look – but that will take time so it could end up being quite **slow**.
4	Do you have the electoral register?	As we discovered when quest-ioning the enquirer, the electoral register is unlikely to give them what they want because they're looking for people with a particular surname. Plenty of genealogical or ancestry or social networking sites could help with this, so there's no shortage of places to look. But it could take a while to track down a good one.	Plenty of possible places to look, so this is pretty **easy** to get started on. After that, though, searching through all the possible places – and probably discovering new ones along the way, could make it pretty **slow**.
5	I'm doing a project on the Westminster Aquarium	This may seem like a pretty straightforward request – but as your student starts searching, they find that the same limited amount of material keeps coming up in lots of places, and it isn't really providing enough to enable them to complete the project.	In view of the enquirer's specific requirement, this turns out to be **hard** and **slow**.

(continued)

Priority	Enquiry	Assessment	Verdict
6	Cash for Parliamentary questions ... Strong & Moral Britain Association ... neo-fascist organizations ... funding ... school governors ... declarations of interest.	This is a very big job; it's probably going to involve a lot of speculative looking up, and quite possibly some phoning round as well. Some parts of it will be more straightforward than others; finding material on the cash-for-questions affair shouldn't be too difficult, for instance, assuming it's had good media coverage. But if the Association is as elusive and secretive as you suspect it is, hunting down the information you need won't be easy and will take time – especially if you have to seek advice from someone else and wait for them to come back to you. On the other hand you could say that the only bit of this three-part query that really matters is what interests school governors have to declare – and it shouldn't prove too difficult to find an accessible source for that.	What the enquirer fundamentally needs is the rules for school governors, and these should be widely available on the web – so pretty **easy** and fairly **quick**. The cash-for-questions aspect will probably be fairly **easy** and quite **quick** – assuming you have access to sources that go back far enough. But the crucial information on the Strong & Moral Britain Association could be very **hard** to find and, with the number of places you might try to look, very **slow** too. So taking the three requests as a whole – and working on the principle that the speed of a convoy is the speed of its slowest vehicle – this enquiry could be very **hard** and very **slow**.
7	I'm trying to find a song called 'When I Would Sing Under the Ocean' [but the title is probably wrong].	The trouble with this enquirer's Chinese whisper is that you're starting off looking for something that doesn't exist, and then once you've realized that, you haven't a clue what the real title is. (Of course, once you do know the correct title, then there are plenty of lists, catalogues, websites – even smartphone apps – that can help you locate it.)	Until you've found some way of discovering the real title, this enquiry will be extremely **hard** and could be very **slow** too. (But once you do know the correct title, tracking the song down should be pretty **easy** and quite **quick**.)

Beware! This is not the right order for everyone. People's assessment of difficulty varies depending on their experience and the environment they work in. A music librarian might put the 'When I Would Sing Under the Ocean' mystery right at the top of the list, for example, because at least they ought to be able to come up with plenty of ideas for tackling it. Or you may decide to split the secretive enquirer's query into three parts, dealing with the rules for school governors first – in which case they may decide that they don't need to know the rest at all. So you should take this section as a guide to the technique, not as the answer to the problem.

If you're doing all the enquiries yourself, your chosen order of priority means that you can start getting answers out from the earliest possible moment, so no one has to wait longer than the difficulty or time-consuming nature of the enquiry merits. If your job is to help the enquirers find the answers for themselves, then this strategy means that everyone gets started as rapidly as possible and you have time to monitor everybody's progress and help wherever necessary.

A compromise solution?

But, unfortunately, even this can't guarantee success. It may be that you really have more to do than you can possibly manage in the time available. In that case, you could find yourself having to compromise on the answer. Do avoid ever saying 'no' if you possibly can, but you have to accept that there will be times when you need to say: 'Yes – but...' The important thing is to try to advance on all fronts – leave everybody with something, rather than some with a complete answer and others with nothing. There are various things you can do to keep to your deadlines.

Suggest sources rather than finding answers

Suggesting sources in which your enquirer can look, rather than finding the answer for them, is an obvious tactic, and enquirers are usually sympathetic if they can see that you're under pressure from other people standing round. But it can be harder to convince them that you're short of time if there's no one else around, no matter how many jobs you are working on for absent enquirers. And don't expect to get any sympathy if you actually list for the enquirer's edification all the other things you have to do – that's your problem, not theirs. If you do have to resort to suggesting sources, make sure that you explain fully to the enquirer how the source works; show them the different indexes available in a printed source, take them through the various menus or buttons on a website or in an electronic document. And invite them to return for further advice if the source doesn't work; don't ever give the impression that you're fobbing them off.

Suggest alternative libraries or information services

Suggesting sources doesn't work with telephone or e-mail enquirers. And, as we saw in Chapter 2, it can be well-nigh impossible to contain a remote enquirer's impatience, no matter how busy you are. So if you can't help them immediately, you could suggest an alternative library or information service that they could try. But again, be as helpful as possible in doing this. Look up the organization's phone number, e-mail address and website, and tell your enquirer exactly what that service can do that you can't. In some cases, merely giving an e-mail enquirer the web address of a relevant institution may be sufficient in itself – especially if its site has a good FAQs section. Beware, though, of directing enquirers to services that they are not entitled to use. Some institutions will accept enquiries only from their members or subscribers; others will want to charge.

Ask for thinking time

An alternative tactic when dealing with telephone or e-mail enquirers is to say: 'Leave it with me; I'll see what I can do.' This buys you valuable time and leaves the enquirer satisfied that you are taking the enquiry seriously. However, you must take the time straight away to go through the full questioning procedure that we discussed in Chapter 1. You must also agree a deadline with the enquirer – and then meet it.

Offer a rough and ready answer

Of course, asking for thinking time merely leaves you with yet another deadline to meet. In that case, an alternative tactic is to offer an instant but partial answer, based on what you have immediately to hand. (This tactic works equally well whether the enquirer is standing in front of you or has got in touch by phone, e-mail or text.) A rough-and-ready answer is usually a briefer one – whatever you can find in a few minutes in readily accessible sources. However, there are some occasions when a rough-and-ready answer can be a longer one. It might take only a few minutes to do a quick search and hand the results over unchecked for the enquirer to go through in detail in their own time. However, if it's normally your job to actually do the research, you may also want to offer to go through the downloaded results yourself later, removing less relevant material and drawing attention to the best sources, when time allows. (This is all part of adding value, and we'll return to it in Chapter 6.)

Progress reports

Whatever strategies you choose to employ to ensure you meet your deadlines, it's important to keep enquirers informed about how you're getting on. It's reassuring to the enquirer, and it shows them that you're being open about any difficulties and not trying to pull the wool over their eyes. Although you'll always hope to succeed, progress reports can prepare enquirers for disappointment (and put them in a mood for accepting a compromise answer) if your searching is going badly. You're likely to do this automatically when the enquirer is standing over you, but you should get into the habit of doing it for absent enquirers too. Whether you're delivering good news or bad, making progress reports may seem irksome and time-consuming, but it undoubtedly pays customer relations dividends.

Plan B

So if you have drawn a blank at every turn, is this the end of the road? Certainly not – although you are now probably going to have to rethink the task and discuss alternative strategies with your enquirer. Sometimes you can anticipate this difficulty. If you work in a specialist information service and a regular user happens to ask you something outside your organization's core business, then you'll probably know straight away that you don't have the resources to answer it in-house. You may even be able to judge that the enquiry is so esoteric and so specific that it might not be in a published source at all, and that locating expert advice is the only solution. So if you do suspect from the outset that you're going to have difficulty answering a particular enquiry, this is the time when you need to bring in the fourth characteristic that we considered in Chapter 3 in addition to focus, dynamism and complexity: viability.

Saying 'no' positively

With so much information now available, in print, online and in electronic documents, is there any excuse for failing to find an answer? Sometimes. Your enquirer may decide that the information is just not worth the cost of using a charged-for service or hiring an independent information professional. You may decide that you can't afford to invest the time on a speculative and possibly fruitless attempt to find a source that might be able to help. No matter how much technology you surround yourself with, and no matter how well funded your organization, there are times when you might still have to admit defeat.

But even this doesn't mean saying 'no'. It means exercising ingenuity in helping your enquirer to continue travelling hopefully instead of hitting a cul-de-sac. It means thinking positively about what you can still do. Remember the technique you used when your mind went blank in Chapter 3? You said 'I'm sure I can help', and indeed you still can – although by now not necessarily in the way your enquirer expected.

Preparing your enquirer for disappointment

So it's probably just as well to start lowering your enquirer's expectations as soon as you realize there are going to be difficulties. This is where the progress reports mentioned earlier really come in useful. You'll be in a much better position to help your enquirer if they're already aware that you are having problems and are starting to think about what sort of alternative answer would do. In your dialogue with the enquirer at this stage, you again each have something to contribute. Your job is to say what's feasible, and your enquirer needs to say what's acceptable as an answer.

An enquirer who's there with you can probably see that things aren't going too well – but it's a bit more challenging if you have to deliver disappointing news by phone or e-mail. As soon as they hear your voice, or see your message in their inbox, they're quite likely to assume that you're coming back with the answer – so you need to let them down gently. Try to have at least some positive news to deliver first – supply what little information you have been able to find, or at the very least report positively on where you've looked. And when you do come to break the bad news, try to couch it in terms of needing to consult the enquirer on how to carry the enquiry forward, rather than simply delivering the bald message that you can't find anything.

What you can do to save the situation at this stage will depend on what exactly your enquirer wants the information for. As we discovered in Chapter 1, people rarely want information merely to satisfy idle curiosity – they nearly always have a purpose in asking. This means that you can sometimes accommodate their needs by providing an alternative answer – less specific than the one they asked for, for example, but almost as helpful in enabling them to reach the conclusion they seek or put forward the argument they want to promote. So what could you try?

Asking authors or editors

Whether you're doing the searching yourself or advising a student in their researches, it's a really good idea to keep a note of the authors of nearly relevant books, articles or (expert) blogs, or the editors of what seem like appropriate journals (whether printed or web-based). So even if you draw a blank with the documents you scrutinize, you still have the option of contacting the author in the hope that they can advise you on more specialized sources. For reasons we've already discussed in Chapter 4, it's almost certainly best to use a professionally edited source for this purpose if you can, rather than just going blindly onto the web. There are plenty of *Who's Who*-type publications that cover writers, but the trouble is that sources of this kind are always highly selective in who they include, and aren't necessarily particularly up to date; so an alternative would be to use the book's publisher as a go-between.

Actually this isn't an ideal solution either, because professional authors (as opposed to enthusiasts) are often reluctant to enter into correspondence, and publishers tend to be protective of their authors too. It partly depends on what kind of author it is. If it's a jobbing writer who makes their living from churning out non-fiction books they're unlikely to be very keen to help. But if it's a specialist in the relevant field – an academic, say – they might be much more willing to advise. Contacting authors of articles in specialist journals or blogs, or the editors of those journals or blogs, can be more fruitful. Driven by their own enthusiasm, they may be more committed to their subject than a commercial writer or publisher would be.

Another alternative might be to scrutinize any bibliographies you find in the publications you try, or likely links on the websites you visit, to see if they can lead you to more detailed sources that your enquirer might be able to see in a specialist library or borrow through a document supply service. (See Chapter 8 for examples of sources and services that can help you with this.)

Suggesting a compromise answer

If neither you nor your enquirer can find any sources that provide the complete answer required, and your deadline is looming, now's the time to start considering a compromise answer – one that's less detailed or less up to date than the enquirer would ideally like. But this must be a joint decision between you and the enquirer with (as we've seen earlier) you saying what's feasible and the enquirer saying what's acceptable. Let's think about possible compromise answers to a couple of our sample enquiries.

There just might not be enough time to undertake a full analysis of all the migration figures for Wales from the mass of statistical data available online. So will the enquirer settle for a pre-packaged digest of the headline figures from the relevant government agency, ready to download in a spreadsheet, plus a handful of articles that explain the trends in brief? You may have been the one to find this material, but it's for the enquirer to say whether it will do in the circumstances.

The student doing the Westminster Aquarium enquiry may simply not have found enough material to sustain their project, but in their searching they should at least have encountered a great deal of tangential material along the way. So is this the time for them to return to their tutor and negotiate a change in the brief – broadening it out, perhaps, to put the Aquarium in the context of other forms of popular Victorian entertainment, on which plenty of material should by now be available? Or if there isn't time to do this – students so frequently only seem to come to the library when their deadline is looming – can you both at least revisit the reading list associated with the project, and try to deduce from the titles listed there what might be an acceptable way of extending the brief?

But beware! Whatever you decide to do at this stage of any enquiry, you've changed the agenda to suit yourself. So be especially sensitive to your enquirer's reaction, to make sure that the suggested change also suits them. Your enquirer will not be impressed if you try to present a less than satisfactory answer as a lovely surprise.

Buying the information in

Realistically, purchasing the information your enquirer needs, as opposed to finding it within resources that you already have, is rarely a viable option. But it would be unwise to rule it out altogether. Many library users are accustomed to the idea of paying a modest charge to get hold of a licensed copy of a crucial journal article, for example. Or an academic with a research grant for the project they're working on may have been required to reserve some part of that money specifically for information purchase. And if your job is to undertake research on behalf of a specialist organization, using a commercial database with a corporate credit card, or even employing an independent specialist information professional, may be more cost-effective than simply carrying on searching through ever less and less likely sources in the hope of achieving a breakthrough.

Of course, if you find yourself regularly having to buy in information to meet the needs of particular enquirers, that's the time to consider whether you shouldn't instead be investing in your own resources to meet what is clearly an ongoing requirement. (More on this in Chapter 6.) These are also crucial decisions that you will have to take when you're initially planning the kind of enquiry service most appropriate for your organization. (We'll return to that in Chapter 7.)

Looking for outside help

If you've got to this stage and you're still stuck for a solution, there's probably no option left but to refer the enquiry somewhere else. Before you take that final decision, though, do make sure you really have exhausted all the in-house possibilities. If you're in a public library, is there a more experienced colleague who happens to be working in a back office at the moment, or a specialist at a bigger branch, whose brains you might be able to pick? If you're helping a student or academic in a college library, have you thought of library subject specialists, who may only occasionally take turns on the desk but are otherwise on call to assist with tricky enquiries within their particular discipline? Or can the student go back to their tutor for further guidance at this stage – including discussing whether the assignment is realistic at all? And if you're a researcher in a specialist organization, are you sure you've tapped all the available in-house expertise away from your own information centre? (And do you have know-how files to help you to do this? We'll come back to that in Chapter 7.)

If, after all this, you're satisfied that you really don't have anything in-house that might provide the answer, that's the time to think about seeking outside help. This offers you lots of scope; there are thousands of sources you could consider, and plenty of places you can look to identify them. But seeking outside help usually imposes delays on the answer and, again as we've already discovered, you frequently don't realize that you're in difficulties until the deadline is looming.

There are hundreds of possible sources that can lead you to outside help on every conceivable topic, and you will be very unlucky indeed if you can't find anywhere at all to direct your enquirer to. (Have a look at some of the Starter Sources featured in Chapter 8; *most* of them can lead you to further sources of help.) Seeking outside help also has the advantage of sticking to the enquirer's agenda, whereas if you suggest a substitute answer, you inevitably shift the agenda to suit yourself. And besides the delay, going outside may mean that you can no longer necessarily guarantee the attention and courtesy that you are of course giving your own enquirer.

But if you do decide that you need to seek outside help, how do you decide where to go? We've already seen how imagining the final answer can get you started on possible sources to try. Now, faced with the task of referring the enquiry somewhere else, there's another hypothetical question you need to ask yourself – and this time it's:

Who really needs to know this?

In other words, what kind of organization just couldn't function if it didn't have this information? Whose job would be on the line if they couldn't tackle an enquiry like this? That's the sort of contact you need to locate, and finding one can frequently be pretty straightforward; you have the subject of the enquiry so you just need to look up an organization that specializes in it. But sometimes you have to exercise a little imagination in determining what kind of organization or person that might be. Let's see how the technique might work with some of the most intransigent of our seven sample enquiries.

Enquiry	Who really needs to know this?
I'm doing a project on the Westminster Aquarium.	Frustrated at their failure to find sufficient detail to satisfy the assignment on what must at first have seemed a fairly straightforward topic, the student should at least have discovered by now where the building was. In response, you will probably be aware – or could speculate – that the local studies library, archive or record office for the area concerned may well be able to provide more detailed material from their original records.
Can you confirm whether the Strong & Moral Britain Association is linked with neo-fascist organizations?	If it's the kind of organization your enquirer suspects, then it probably won't be particularly forthcoming with information about itself – either in any publication or if you try to phone on the enquirer's behalf and ask it directly. But working on the principle of 'Know thine enemy', the kind of organization that would really need to know about an outfit like this would be one that was opposed to it – so try looking for anti-fascist organizations or equality bodies that might be able to advise you.
I'm trying to find a song called 'When I Would Sing Under the Ocean' [but the title is probably wrong].	Logically, nobody *really needs* to know this song title because it doesn't exist. So you're going to have to rely on someone, somewhere, making an intuitive leap and working out what the title must really be. A light opera or musical enthusiast might be the kind of person to look for – and that could include many knowledgeable music librarians. So, to increase the odds of finding that special person, why not crowdsource it? It only takes one person out of potentially thousands on a relevant discussion list or social network group to work out that it's probably 'When I Was King of the Beotians' and the query is instantly unblocked.

Of course, having found what looks like the right organization to help, there's still no guarantee that it will co-operate. So keep your request sensible – ask for only the minimum amount of help you need in order to move forward. It also helps if you can avoid the telephone merry-go-round that you risk encountering if you simply phone the organization's switchboard. So try using some of the Starter Sources detailed in Chapter 8 to see first if an organization has a library or information service, where you could reasonably expect a more sympathetic response than you might get from the reception desk. Failing that, see if the organization has a public relations department – the bit that's paid to be nice to outsiders. Above all, do prepare the ground for your enquirer; don't just send them off on a wild goose chase. If they do try somewhere else on your recommendation and get a dusty answer in response, that will reflect badly on you.

Coming next – adding value...

Let's continue on a more positive note. This book is about success, after all. But successful enquiry answering doesn't simply mean handing the answer over with no further comment. It's about making sure that what you provide is the best available, presented to your enquirer in the most helpful way possible. So in the next chapter, we'll look at how to add value to your answers.

To recap . . .

■ **Distinguish between vital and urgent tasks.**
■ **Prioritize your enquiries on the easy/hard, quick/slow principle.**
■ **Make sure that any compromise solution really meets your enquirer's needs.**
■ **If you're not sure where to go for help, ask yourself who really needs to know it.**

CHAPTER 6

Success! Now let's add some value

Presenting your answer well is part of the job

> **In this chapter you'll find out how to:**
>
> - **quality check your answer**
> - **present it effectively in writing, orally or visually**
> - **make sure you've observed copyright and licensing requirements**
> - **confirm that the enquirer is satisfied**
> - **gather performance data.**

'It ain't what you do, it's the way that you do it,' goes the old Ella Fitzgerald song. True enough – but the real wisdom is in the last line: 'That's what gets results.'

Whether you're helping members of the public, mentoring students or providing a full research service to a specific organization, there's every reason to take pride in the answers you provide. This is partly for your personal satisfaction, but it's also really good customer relations. A service that looks and sounds good inspires customer confidence and wins repeat business; one that doesn't risks losing that confidence, resulting in declining business and possibly even closure. In helping people find the information they want, you haven't been doing something easy, you've been doing something highly skilled – so don't spoil it with a weak finish.

Obviously, presenting your answer well matters when you're providing finished research results. But it's just as important to be clear and concise – and to prioritize the information you provide – when you're advising enquirers on sources or search techniques. Presentation also matters when you're advising on a transaction – how to request a document, access an electronic resource, use an online service, follow a procedure. Whatever the circumstances, presentation isn't an optional extra; it's an essential ingredient for the future development of your service.

Quality checking your answer

But just before you present your answer, it's wise to have one final quality check – just to make sure you haven't missed anything important or accidentally done something silly. As with so many of these stages in the enquiry answering process, it may seem a bit tedious – but it's far better if you discover a howler before delivering the answer rather than letting the enquirer find it afterwards. So here are a few thoughts on final things to check.

Have you really answered it?

Remember that you have an implied contract with your enquirer as a result of all the careful questioning you undertook at the start of the process. So now go back and check the recorded wording of the enquiry carefully. Do this for two reasons – firstly, because you waste your enquirer's time if you find that you've allowed yourself to be unconsciously diverted during the course of your researches. Printed and electronic sources are full of diverting side alleys, and you need to be sure that you haven't been tempted. Secondly, you need to check because enquirers are quite capable of changing the agenda while you are searching without bothering to tell you. Remember the problems we encountered in Chapter 1, trying to find out what the enquirer really wanted in the first place? Unfortunately, it doesn't stop there. While you are busy trying to find the answer, your enquirer is still thinking about the question, and probably coming up with all sorts of supplementary information that they'd like as well. Or they may have been pursuing their own researches in parallel to yours, and have already come up with the answer themselves. Annoying as this may be, you have to be tolerant. After all, it's just a job for you, but it might be personally very important for them.

What to leave out – what to keep in

We worried about providing too much information as early as Chapter 1. But it's now, while you're preparing to present your answer, that it really matters. You may well have found similar information from several different sources. This could be because you were unhappy with the level of detail or reliability of the first source you used, and wanted to see whether you could improve on it in another one. Or because you found several articles or news items on the same subject, with huge overlaps between them. Or half a dozen different organizations that you could refer your enquirer to, because you hadn't been able to find the information in-house.

But there's no rule that says you have to supply them all. As the quantity of available information continues to grow, enquirers will be looking to library and information professionals for their expertise not only in finding the right answer but also in judging which is the best version of the right answer. All information work is about choices – choosing what sources to buy, choosing what index entries to create for them, choosing what to leave out when you write abstracts of them. Why should enquiry work be any different?

So what sorts of things do you need to consider when deciding what to keep in your final answer? Here are a few quality indicators that you could use:

Is the source authoritative? Who is the author? If it's an individual, do they appear to be appropriately qualified in the subject and to have followed a relevant career path? If it's an organization, what kind is it? Is it official, regulated or a centre of excellence?

What is the source's agenda? It's probably fair to say that all information reflects the author's values, which will in turn dictate what they've chosen to emphasize or ignore – whether that author is an individual or an organization. So are you satisfied that you understand what the author's agenda is, and are you ready to explain that to the enquirer – based on the facts, not your own value judgement?

Have you seen it referred to several times already? Has the same source come up in different bibliographies, retrieved database records or search engine results? (Actually as we've seen in Chapter 4 this is no longer necessarily a foolproof test. The web is a viral medium and it may be that the same misleading document has been copied from location to location to location unchecked. So you do need to satisfy yourself about the source's authority and agenda as well.)

Will it allow your enquirer to... Take a decision, make a recommendation or take action? As we've already seen in Chapter 1, enquirers almost always ask for information for a specific purpose, not merely to satisfy idle curiosity. So you do need to ensure that what you intend to provide really will meet the enquirer's practical requirements.

Information versus references

Of course, there will be times when you genuinely don't feel qualified to make decisions of this kind – in highly technical subjects such as medicine or law, for instance. But even then you can still opt for offering complete texts of only some of the sources, and providing references to the others. That way, you've minimized the amount that your enquirer has to read and, if you're providing your answer on paper, then you've also been kind to trees.

Whatever you finally decide to provide, you should always tell your enquirer where the information has come from. It may be tempting to keep these details to yourself, in a misguided attempt to ensure that the enquirer remains dependent on you. But resist the temptation. Firstly, it's a very unprofessional practice for one whose job is providing information from public domain sources. Secondly, it's all too easy for an enquirer to go to another library or information service that is prepared to source its information. And thirdly, if your enquirer subsequently comes back for further details, it's extremely embarrassing if you can't remember where the information came from in the first place.

Presenting your answer – orally

Now you're finally ready to present it. So just take a few moments to decide how you're going to do it. After all, you don't want to spoil the climax, do you?

Preparing your answer

You may think that presenting an answer orally is just like normal conversation and doesn't need any prior preparation. Well, it isn't and it does. An oral answer needs to be as carefully structured and as clearly laid out as a written one. It's quite likely, for instance, that your enquirer will be taking notes while you deliver your oral answer, so it's only sensible to make their note taking as easy as possible by setting out your message logically. If you're responding by phone, remember too that it will probably take a few seconds for the person at the other end to get onto your wavelength. So use those seconds to introduce yourself, say where you're calling from and remind the enquirer what they asked for. Then check that they've got a pen and paper handy. Then give them the answer.

There are a couple of storytelling techniques that might help you to do this. The first is the one beloved of trainers: tell them what you're going to tell them; tell them; then tell them what you've told them. And the second technique is one that journalists classically use: the inverted pyramid. When you read a detective novel, you want the apex of the pyramid – who did it – to be kept back to the very last page. But when you read a news story, you want the denouement to come first. So a news story will start with the climax, then give important supporting detail and finally include less relevant ancillary information at the bottom. This is so a reader can leave the story at any point, satisfied that they have the most important information, and it also enables an editor to chop off a story for length at the bottom, secure in the knowledge that they haven't excised anything important. Either of these techniques can be useful for delivering oral answers – so let's see how they both might work if you were phoning through the answer to the very simple enquiry: 'What is Marks & Spencer's pre-tax profit?'

First of all, using the 'tell them' technique:

Introduce yourself.	Hello, is that Mr Sampson? This is Delilah Milton from the Ghaza Mills Library.
Tell them what you're going to tell them.	You asked me to find Marks & Spencer's current pre-tax profit, and I have the information for you if you're ready.
Tell them.	The current figures come from their half year results, published on 8 November. They show the underlying profit before tax at £315.2 million and the profit before tax at £320.5 million.
Tell them what you've told them.	So just to confirm, those are the two headline figures as published in a press release on the company's website on the day the results came out.
Give the enquirer a chance to respond.	Is there anything else I can help you with at this stage?
And add some value.	Would you like me to text or e-mail those figures over to you? And do you need the definition of the distinction between profit and underlying profit? The release includes all the other headline figures and comparisons with the previous period. Would it help if I sent you the web address of the release, so you can extract whatever other figures you might need?

Using this technique, you can confine your actual answer to the specific piece of information the enquirer asked for, while making certain at the same time that they really have taken that information in. But what happens to all the other related information that the enquirer didn't ask for but which you will inevitably have discovered at the same time? Using the 'tell them' technique you can at least offer it without necessarily having prepared it in advance. But with the inverted pyramid technique you need to have all the available information ready to report straight away, and allow the enquirer to cut you off once they have enough.

So now here's the answer using the 'inverted pyramid' technique. Again, you'd introduce yourself, to give the enquirer an opportunity to gather their thoughts. After that, your oral report might go as follows:

Climax	Marks & Spencer's pre-tax profit, which you asked for, is currently £320.5 million. But the company also includes a second figure for underlying profit before tax, which is slightly lower at £315.2 million. This is from the company's own half-year results, published on its website on 8 November. Shall I tell you what the company says about the distinction between the two figures?
Supporting information	It explains that underlying results are consistent with how the business is measured internally. Adjustments to underlying profit include profit and loss on property disposals, investment property impairment charges, fair value movements on financial instruments and embedded derivatives, one-off pension credits and strategic programme costs which are not considered normal operating costs of the business. There is some more that might be of interest to you in relation to their current profits, if you'd like to hear it?
Ancillary information	In the same period last year both these figures – profit and underlying profit – were shown as being higher at £348.6 million. But despite the reduction in profit this time, group sales, excluding value-added tax, have increased by 2.4% to £4.7 billion. In his statement the chief executive says that the company took a decision to invest in giving customers better value, choosing not to pass on the full extent of the increases in commodity prices. Would it help if I e-mailed you the web address where can find all this information, in case you'd like to study it further for yourself?

As before, you'd give the enquirer a chance to respond – but this time you'd pause at each point in the pyramid, giving them exactly the same opportunity to stop you as the reader of a news story has. You may of course argue that the enquirer didn't ask for all this ancillary stuff. But it does offer valuable clues as to why the figures are as they are, and it's all part of adding value to your answer – if the enquirer wants it.

Two final points. Firstly, in the ancillary information, you're not actually saying that there's a connection between the company's decision to hold down prices and its reduced profits; you're not qualified to do that. But common sense would suggest that there may be, so it's only right to draw the information to the enquirer's attention and leave them to come to their own conclusion. And secondly, although in this instance you didn't offer to e-mail over the web address until the end, you did give the source of the information right at the beginning. As with any enquiry work, the source of your information isn't an ancillary detail; it's part of the climax.

Recommending sources or search strategies

These two techniques – 'tell them' and 'inverted pyramid' – work just as effectively when you're delivering information face-to-face. And they also work when you're supporting students or members of the public in their searching as opposed to doing the actual research for them. With the 'tell them' technique, you may decide to begin by outlining all the available sources to use, then explain in a little more detail what each of these sources will do, and finally review them, perhaps with a recommendation on the best sources to try first. Using the 'inverted pyramid', you might begin by recommending a couple of the best sources, then outline the ones to turn to next if necessary, and finally list the others that you don't recommend. (And here, of course, you are entitled to advise and make recommendations, because information sources are your area of expertise.)

Giving instructions

If ever there was a time when you needed to plan your oral delivery of information carefully, it's when you're giving instructions – how to reserve a book, order an electronic article, pay a fine, navigate through a portal or round a discovery tool, set up a feed, use an advanced search engine, understand the structure of a website. It's not too bad when the enquirer is with you, and you can watch over their shoulder and take them through the process one stage at a time. But it's much trickier when you're trying to guide them by phone. So here are some things to think about.

First of all, take everything step by step; don't be tempted to give more than one instruction at a time. Instead, give the first instruction, tell the enquirer what should happen as a result, and wait until they've confirmed that it has. Of course, that assumes that what you expect to happen actually does happen. If the enquirer says that it hasn't, you're flying blind because you can't see what's come up on their screen and it can take ages to find out what's caused the problem.

So a better technique is to do the task yourself while explaining how to do it – right up to the point where the enquirer needs to put in their actual request. That way you won't accidentally miss a step out and – hopefully – if something does go wrong it will go wrong on your screen as well as the enquirer's, at the same point in the process. However, you do need to make sure that you and the enquirer are starting at the same place; so if necessary, e-mail them the address of the page where you want to start. Obviously, while you're instructing the enquirer you'll be using your own user ID and password and the enquirer will be using theirs; so it's important to ensure that your personal identifier as a member of staff doesn't mean that you can see things on the screen that the enquirer can't or that you go through stages that the enquirer doesn't. But if you still suspect that you and the enquirer are not looking at the same thing – using different browsers, for example – you can ask the enquirer to e-mail you a screenshot so you can see where the problem lies. (And you may have to instruct them in how to do that too.)

Presenting your answer – in writing

Everything that we discussed about presenting answers orally applies to written answers too – only more so. The enquirer can't interrupt and query things so easily in writing – even when you're using a comparatively interactive medium like texting or instant messaging – because it takes time to type a response and that interrupts the flow of the conversation. So it's important to compose your written answer carefully, using the same storytelling techniques that we looked at earlier and trying to anticipate the points at which the enquirer might raise queries. Let's think about what this might mean for the various ways in which you could deliver written information.

E-mail

E-mail is probably the commonest medium you'll use to deliver written answers, and it has a lot going for it. There are no restrictions on the length of an e-mail and it's easy to include links and attachments within it. Whether received on a desktop computer, laptop or tablet device, e-mails should be easy to read, with enough text showing in each screen for the enquirer to be able to take in the totality of the answer comparatively easily. But bear in mind that your enquirer might receive the e-mail on a smartphone or other small screen device – so it may help them to read it more easily if you keep your paragraphs short.

E-mail is a relatively informal medium, so it also helps if you keep e-mails friendly. There's a good practical reason for this: you're much less likely either to cause or take offence if you keep your wording conversational. So avoid using formal language in your e-mails and your pre-composed e-mail responses. A more relaxed, conversational style is generally more appropriate, although you may have to develop policies with your management on what degree of informality is acceptable. It's also a good idea to avoid using passive constructions in e-mails; they can come across as bureaucratic and inflexible. And if you do have to deliver disappointing news by e-mail, try to start with a possible solution to the problem. Finally, just before you send it, say it in your head. Are you certain that the enquirer isn't going to interpret it as being unsympathetic, unhelpful or a 'job's worth'? Remember the message in Chapter 2: it's the recipient who decides where to place the emphasis on the words you send – not you.

Attachments

An e-mail with an attachment can often constitute the perfect answer to an enquiry: a report on what you've done and what you've found, backed up by the documentary evidence to support it. But don't assume that your enquirer has ultra-fast broadband. They may be using a mobile internet connection at a comparatively slow speed, or even still be on dial-up. So check first if it's OK to include an attachment, tell them what the file size is, and see if it isn't possible to send them a link instead.

Enhancing electronic documents

With information presented electronically, the number of ways you can enhance it is only limited by your own imagination. If you're sending a **word-processed document**, you can help your enquirer to make sense of a large body of text by adding headlines, subheadings and guiding, and by highlighting the key words or phrases in the text in bold or italic. Finding those words or phrases is easy for you; using the word search facility in your word-processing package or web browser, it takes only a few seconds for you to add an enormous amount of value to the answer. Alternatively, you could copy key paragraphs out of the original text and paste them in at the head of your answer. This allows your enquirer to take in the crucial information immediately, and to read it in its proper context later on – a variant of the 'inverted pyramid' technique.

You can enhance **numeric data** in the same way. If you have downloaded some statistical information to a spreadsheet, then it need be the work of only a few minutes to add value by calculating an average or median for the figures retrieved, or expressing them as percentages for greater clarity, or ranking them. Or you can turn them into a graph, bar or pie chart, usually using software embedded within the spreadsheet package. Make sure you really understand what you're doing, though. It's all too easy for simple mistakes in spreadsheet creation to render figures seriously misleading, if not downright wrong.

As we saw in Chapter 3, **images** are now an immensely valuable source of information. So you can drop images into word-processed documents, or even supply your answer as a presentation or web page if you think that's more appropriate. And as with electronic text, you don't necessarily need to show the whole picture; if one detail is particularly important, crop it out of the main image using standard image-processing software or even simply the image-formatting facility on your word processor or presentation package.

If you're sending **PDF documents**, which you can't easily edit without the right software, you can at least copy key elements – whether text or images – out of the original and paste them into your covering e-mail with appropriate comment.

Two words of warning before you do any of this, though. Make sure your enquirer is fully aware of how your enhanced versions of documents differ from the original – and of course bear in mind that there may be important copyright and licensing limitations that you need to be aware of. (We'll return to these issues later in the chapter.)

Texting

Using the Short Message Service (SMS) on a mobile phone – texting – can be a very effective way of communicating. It's a one-to-one medium that many enquirers, especially students, tend to use heavily and trust, and it can be very user-friendly if used sensitively – so it's potentially good for customer relations. But it imposes limits on how much you can say in so many ways.

Individual SMS messages can be up to 160 characters in length. That's roughly about 26 words (including spaces and punctuation) or perhaps 2–3 sentences. However, it is possible for most phones to break up longer text messages into segments and send them in sequence for the receiving phone to reassemble at the other end. In practice, 6–8 segments is the maximum, and since you need part of the message space for the data to enable the receiving phone to reassemble the message correctly, this reduces the available number of message characters in each segment to around 150 or less. So this means that you can send up to about 900–1200 characters in a 'concatenated' text message, or very roughly 150–200 words – assuming that your enquirer's phone can accept and process messages sent in segments, that is.

On older conventional mobile phones you can rarely see more than about three lines of text at a time and three to four words per line – less if you use long words. You can see a lot more text on smartphones with bigger screens. But it still only amounts to a medium-length paragraph per screen, with not more than about seven words per line if the recipient can't reorientate their screen to receive text in 'landscape' form (i.e. wider than it is high). With any kind of small screen, the enquirer can't rely so much on their peripheral vision to take in the whole message and may have to remember the earlier part of a lengthy message while reading the later. Finally, the characters are quite small and SMS messages come out as a single block of text, so they can sometimes be difficult to read and understand easily and quickly.

However, there are things you can do to overcome some of these limitations. Firstly, keep your sentences and your words as short as possible. (This is actually good practice no matter how you choose to communicate.) Also, don't include more information than you could reasonably put in a single short paragraph of around two to three sentences. Make sure the message is easily understandable, written in plain language and clearly structured. If you have to send web addresses using SMS, shorten them using one of several available shortening tools, both to save your limited message space and to avoid blocking several lines on a tiny screen with a lengthy address. Yet, despite the space limitations, try not to make your messages too terse. Reserve some space for a friendly greeting and sign-off if you can. Having said that, though, it's not a good idea to use other compressions (e.g. cul8r – 'see you later'); you can't be certain the recipient will know what they mean.

Research reports

If you have to provide answers in the form of reports based on desk research then, in addition to all the other value you can add, you need to think about the look and feel of your documents too. Once again, this isn't an optional extra; it's a vital part of promoting your service, keeping it relevant in the eyes of decision-makers, and ensuring that it survives and thrives.

So incorporate your organization's logo, preferred colour palette and fonts into your own reports. Take advice from your professional designer – whether an in-house design team or a retained external consultant. If the budget permits and house style rules allow it, get them to create a variant of your organization's logo incorporating the name of your own service. And look carefully at how professionally designed documents are laid out – particularly those of your own organization but also others if you think it appropriate. Think about features like columns, sidebars, dropped top margins, line spacing, text wrapped round illustrations or graphics, complementary font colours. Most, if not all, of these features that are the professional designer's stock in trade can be replicated on standard word-processing packages. And if you're then able to deliver your report as a PDF, it ensures that all your carefully constructed design elements arrive on your enquirer's computer looking exactly the same as they did when they left yours.

Screen presentations

All these design considerations apply when you need to present answers on screen too. You're not restricted to headings and bullet points when you use presentation packages; you can treat the screen as a blank canvas onto which you can place text, images and objects wherever you like for maximum impact. Look, for example, at the way television presenters show complex information in simple visual form – using a composite image of appropriate elements as a background to a subject like the economy, science or social issues. Facts and figures will be displayed on an appropriate surface – a brick wall for a report on graffiti, a football pitch for a sports report. Again, all of these techniques are replicable using standard presentation software.

But is it worth the effort? That's up to you. It is certainly all too easy to get carried away and concentrate on the presentation to the detriment of the content. But bear in mind that such techniques are tried and tested in the media, and that decision-makers probably have to sit through lots and lots of boring presentations consisting of nothing but headings and bullet points. So if you can create one really compelling design template that you then can use over and over, it could be time well invested in terms of the impact your service makes on its clientele.

Enhancing answers on paper

And let's not forget the humble piece of paper. If you're supplying a photocopy for your enquirer to keep, or if you're faxing the information back, mark the crucial sections. Highlight the relevant paragraph with a marker pen. Put asterisks against the most useful entries in a directory or bibliography. Draw a line down the required column or across the required row of a table of statistics. Put in an arrow head to point out the key component of a diagram. Circle the right place on a map. And, whatever else you do, make sure that the source of your document is clearly cited. Underline it if it's already printed there; write it in if not. These are suggestions, of course, not hard and fast rules. But, as a general principle, do whatever you can to lead your enquirer to the information they want as rapidly and clearly as possible. The cost of doing such things is minuscule, the customer relations value immense.

Copyright, licensing, ethics

There are ethical considerations to bear in mind when manipulating text, numbers or images in this way. Be sure that you make it quite clear what you have done with the version of the document that you finally present to your enquirer, so that they are in no doubt as to how it varies from the original. (And, as always, make sure that you cite the source in full in your answer.)

Just as crucial are copyright and licensing. Put very simply, copyright (including database rights) provides statutory protection for authors, permitting them to exploit their intellectual property in any way they wish and putting strict limits on what others may do with it. Licensing is a contract agreement between the content supplier and purchaser, specifying in detail what the user may and may not do with that particular content. As a general rule, licences should extend what is permissible under copyright law, not further restrict it. Copyright and licensing can affect activities such as lending, copying, scanning, faxing, downloading – and enquiry answering.

So before you engage in any value-added activity of this kind, be sure that you understand the terms on which the content concerned has been supplied to you. If the licence forbids supply of copies to a third party – for example, to enquirers who are not members of your college – then, no matter how much you may regret the missed opportunity, you must not do it. As a general principle, in fact, you should make sure that you understand all the copyright and licensing requirements under which your library or information service operates before you start any enquiry work. Copying in all media has now become so easy that publishers are understandably more and more vigilant about infringements. So if you're in any doubt about what you're allowed to do, seek advice. Nothing could be worse for your customer relations than promising something that the rules don't subsequently allow you to deliver.

Has the answer arrived – and does the enquirer like it?

Yet again, when the enquirer is with you and you've been working on an enquiry together, it's relatively easy to tell when it's finally finished and whether the enquirer is satisfied with the answer. To put it bluntly, you ask them and they tell you. But, as we've seen so often already, it's all very different when the enquirer is somewhere else.

So first of all, has the answer actually arrived where it was supposed to? Not much doubt if it's something simple and brief that you phone through. But if the enquirer doesn't answer, you might have to leave a message with their colleague or on their voicemail, asking them to call you back. And do you risk actually leaving the answer in a voicemail message? It may be confidential and something that the enquirer doesn't want to risk others in their organization finding out. Of course, if you've done your job properly (see Chapter 2), you'll have at least two means of contacting them. But whatever the outcome, it's likely to mean a delay before you can finally sign the enquiry off.

And if you're replying using a text-based medium – e-mail, text, instant messaging – you have little guarantee that the answer has arrived safely, and none at all that the enquirer is satisfied. Asking for a 'delivery' or a 'read' receipt for an e-mail tells you nothing either; it simply means that someone, somewhere, opened it. It doesn't tell you if it's the right person, and certainly not whether it's what they wanted. So if you don't hear back from the enquirer with an acknowledgement pretty soon, contact them again to check – possibly using the same medium as you did before but preferably using a different one. Phone if you originally e-mailed; leave a text on their mobile if you got no response from their landline. If this all seems terribly tedious – a bit 'belt and braces' – remember that it's better than having a discontented customer on your hands. They might never tell you about their discontent, so you'll never be able to take remedial action. But they may well tell lots of their friends, potentially damaging your reputation in the process.

Sign-off: what can we learn from this enquiry?

With the enquirer satisfied and the enquiry signed off your task is nearly over. But before you finally file it away, there's still one more piece of value you can add – value to your own organization. If the enquiry was anything other than routine, there are some really useful lessons to be learned from it – plus quite possibly new information sources to consider and new services that you could introduce as a result.

So take some time to review the completed enquiry. Assess it for its difficulty and the time it took. Look carefully at the sources and delivery media you used; there are likely to be some new ones, and you need to consider whether or not it might be worth purchasing or subscribing to them. You may possibly have contacted some useful new organizations as well; you'll need to decide how to record them so you can benefit from their expertise again in the future. The enquiry may even have suggested to you an entirely new service that you could offer as a result, in which case you will have a lot of thinking to do, deciding how best to introduce and manage it. Completing an enquiry successfully isn't the end; it's the start of the next phase in your enquiry service. So let's look at some of these considerations in more detail.

How successful were you?

Just as we said in Chapter 1 that you mustn't accept a vague deadline, so you shouldn't tolerate an imprecise measure of success either. It's all too easy for a complacent colleague to record as 'successful' an enquiry that a more conscientious one might regard as only partially successful. Taken to its extreme, this could result in the more conscientious one ending up with a poorer annual appraisal report than the complacent one (and even a lower salary increase), simply because they were more honest and realistic in recording their degree of success.

So instead, you should go for more objective measures. If you've been meticulous in agreeing with the enquirer precisely what you were going to do for them, and had worked out exactly what the final answer would look like, then it should be possible to apply one of three measures of success – complete, partial or compromise.

Complete success means that you have provided an answer that met the enquirer's needs in every respect. In the case of the cash-for-questions query, for example, this would mean that you had: found some useful news coverage of the cash-for-questions affair that either mentioned your enquirer's brother or specifically eliminated him; discovered how the Strong & Moral Britain Association was funded and whether or not it was associated with neo-fascist organizations; and been able to provide some authoritative guidelines on what obligations school governors faced regarding declaration of other interests. Anything less than this, and you would probably have to record the degree of success as 'partial'.

Partial success means that you have been able to find some of what the enquirer wants, but not all. You may, for example, have come up with some figures on migration patterns in Wales which showed general trends over a period for the whole country, but not necessarily the degree of detail that the enquirer would have liked – nothing on specific movements into and out of Glamorgan, for example. In this case, you've certainly provided an answer that will get the enquirer started, but not enough to enable them to finish their task to their satisfaction; so you've probably referred them somewhere else as well. (We'll deal with recording referrals in a moment.)

Compromise means that you and the enquirer have together agreed on an answer that was not exactly what they originally wanted, but which is an acceptable alternative nevertheless. In the Westminster Aquarium query, you may have agreed to supplement the paltry and repetitive offerings you can provide on the Aquarium itself with background on Victorian entertainments, or rival attractions of the period, just to enable the enquirer to complete the project to their supervisor's satisfaction. This is not an ideal outcome, and you must of course have agreed it with the enquirer. But it's about as close to an admission of failure as you should ever allow your enquiry service to come.

Should you ever need to record that you were completely unsuccessful? Hopefully not. Remember the promise you gave when you were starting to think about how you would answer the enquiry back in Chapter 3? 'I'm sure I can help' was what you said – and so you can, even if you and the enquirer eventually had to compromise on what kind of answer would be acceptable. If you ever felt that you had to record a result as 'unsuccessful', that would probably just mean that the enquiry wasn't finished yet. (Note, too, that we haven't talked about referrals; we'll come back to those in a moment.)

Was the enquirer satisfied?

As well as recording your success objectively, you should also seek as objective a measure as possible of the enquirer's satisfaction with the result.

You could do this by using the same words as before – complete, partial, compromise – and inviting your enquirer to choose one of them. That would give a direct comparison between your and the enquirer's perceptions of success, which could provide valuable management data showing how your service is regarded and perhaps revealing patterns indicating where you might need improvements.

Or you could ask the enquirer a question like: 'On a scale of 1 to 5, how satisfied were you with the answer you received (1 being dissatisfied and 5 being completely satisfied)?' If you use this method, you (or your management) will need to think carefully about what range of scores to offer. A scale of 1 to 10 could give you useful percentage scores, but it's a very long scale for your enquirer to get their head round. But if you use 1 to 5, that allows the enquirer to sit on the fence by choosing 3. Using 1 to 4 would enable you to analyse satisfaction by quartiles – but it's so close to the 3 to 1 scale implicit in the 'complete, partial, compromise' measure that you might as well use that instead. So no answers here – just some food for thought.

While your measure of success is hopefully as objective as possible, your enquirer's perception could be a great deal more subjective. You'll encounter some enquirers who are effusively appreciative of answers that actually took you very little time to find, while others may be distinctly unimpressed no matter how much effort you've had to go to. The moral from this is that you shouldn't rely on too little enquirer satisfaction data; only a large dataset can begin to reduce the subjectivity of individual enquirer responses.

How long did it take to answer?

In recording this, you'll need to consider whether the time it took was pretty much what you would have expected, or whether it took longer. If it did take longer, then was this because it was more difficult than you expected, or just more time-consuming? These are not necessarily the same thing, and it comes back to the easy/quick, hard/slow decisions you had to take when you were deciding on the working timetable for prioritizing your enquiries (Chapter 5). It is vitally important to know how long enquiries take to answer because time is money, and if there's a pattern to the difficult and/or lengthy enquiries then that raises implications about the appropriateness and value of the sources and delivery media you're using. Perhaps you need to invest in something new – and maybe you'll be able to offer some useful new services as a result. (We'll come back to this a little later on.)

Did you meet the deadline?

There are only two possible answers to this – yes or no. Nothing else will do, and if you're recording 'no' a lot in this box then, again, you need to do some serious thinking about why, and what you can do to improve your 'yes' score. If you had to negotiate more time (you didn't just present a late answer without warning the enquirer that that was going to happen, did you?), then you need to record your reasons – not just to get you off the hook but so you can decide what service improvements are needed to try to prevent it happening again. It may well be that the enquiry took a long time because you just didn't know what would be the best sources or delivery media to get you started. Well, now you do. So record them, and make use of what you have learned the next time a similar enquiry comes up. (We'll come back to this in a moment.)

Did you have to refer the enquiry elsewhere?

If you recorded partial success or a compromise outcome, then that may well mean that you also referred the enquiry to another organization. This should trigger a whole range of questions about how your service might be able to change and develop as a result. If it's an organization that you have never used before then, firstly, how did you discover it? If it was through a directory (print or electronic) then does that mean that that directory is actually more useful than you previously thought it was? Have you checked the new organization's website to find out what else it can offer? Is that site worth bookmarking or adding to your list of 'favourites' for future reference? If so, where is the best place to put it in your 'favourites' classification?

And what about the organization itself? When you contacted it (You did contact it, didn't you? You didn't just leave the enquirer to make a cold call?) were the staff both helpful and useful (not necessarily the same thing)? If they were both helpful and useful, did they help out of goodwill? Or does the organization have an agenda to pursue? If the former, then you should certainly be grateful, but shouldn't necessarily rely on that goodwill persisting if you keep going back to the same organization time and time again. At some point, you may need to decide what kind of long term relationship you want to have with it (see below). If it has an agenda, then that's fine just as long as you're clear what that agenda is. If you went looking for expert help on the health effects of radiation, for example, you may get exactly the same information from both the Health Protection Agency (a government body) and Friends of the Earth (an environmental pressure group) – but they might put different interpretations on that information. Or if you contact an industry or trade organization, you'll need to know whether it's on the producer or consumer side of the fence, or whether it represents employers or employees – something which may not necessarily be obvious from its name.

Melodramatic as it may seem, you'll also need to know whether the organizations you contact are discreet. If an enquirer approaches an organization on your advice, and subsequently finds themselves bombarded with unsolicited communications from it, then they're likely to be upset with you at the intrusion on their privacy and, quite possibly, the infringement of data protection as well. And if your approach to the organization or – even worse – your enquirer's approach becomes public without your or their consent, then you're in even bigger trouble. You may of course have redress against the organization under data protection law, but by that time the damage will have been done. So the moral is: ask immediately whether the organization handles all enquiries in confidence. This still doesn't guarantee that it really will do so, of course – but at least you have it on record that you did ask and that it gave you an assurance.

Assuming that your referral organization has passed all these tests, you'll finally need to consider your long-term relationship with it. It may be a trade association or professional body that offers a charged-for enquiry or advice service, which you might consider subscribing to. This is a big decision, of course, with implications for your budget, so it's not to be undertaken lightly. But you can't undertake it at all unless you have recorded the enquiry properly in the first place.

Did you discover any useful new resources?

Sometimes a source you already subscribe to but have never really had the time to get to know properly will turn out to be ideal for a particular kind of enquiry that has always foxed you in the past. So when you do discover a useful new source – whether print or electronic – make sure you have procedures in place for recording it properly. You may opt, for example, for a customized know-how or FAQs file. The form it takes will depend on the nature of the searching aids you have already chosen to develop for your service. It could simply be a regularly updated list on paper that you keep at the enquiry desk, but this seems a less and less satisfactory solution when there are so many more effective and flexible networked methods you could employ. So consider instead creating an in-house database – whether using a database package or simply a word processor – that you can post to your organization's intranet. Instantly updatable at any time, it should also enable you to create automatic links to any websites or e-mail addresses or centrally stored electronic documents that you include in it.

If it's on your intranet, everybody in the organization can have access to it. If it's just a file on your network drive, then you'll probably need to make it read-only, so that only authorized people can make changes after due consideration and so your indexing remains up to standard. However, you could consider using a social tool – perhaps one already available through your federated search or discovery system – thereby allowing other people in the organization to add their own comments. An intranet-based FAQ or know-how file, reflecting your resources and services and including live links to internal sources of information or expertise, could in fact turn out to be one of the most valuable resources you could provide.

When you discover a new source that you don't currently have, then you need to consider whether it's worth purchasing or subscribing to. If you decide that it is, you should also consider which delivery medium would be most useful for you. (Sometimes content vendors insist on a combined print and online package, even if one of these two would have been sufficient on its own.) You'll also need to examine any copyright or licensing requirements, to ensure that you are entitled to exploit it in the way you want. If, for example, you intend to network the new source direct to your users throughout the organization, then there are likely to be cost implications, because licence fees often vary depending on how many desks you intend to serve.

Finally, you should have procedures in place for telling both your colleagues and your users about new services that you can offer as a result of new sources acquired. And remember, too, that it should be that way round. Your enquirers aren't interested in sources, but in outcomes. You could use something as simple as a regularly e-mailed current awareness bulletin or newsletter – but even better would be to put these details on your corporate intranet, perhaps using software that supports collaborative working and allows users to comment on how useful they have found specific sources to be.

Developing and maintaining services like these can all take time that you may feel you can ill afford when there are other pressing enquiries to be answered. But do try to make time to investigate new sources and to ensure you are fully exploiting the ones you already have. It will pay enormous dividends, and will mean that you will be able to provide an even better enquiry service in the future.

Coming next...

Throughout this book so far, we've tended to assume that you're working in a multipurpose library or information service serving a fairly large community – members of the public, students at a college or the staff of a public or private sector organization. If so, then you'll have colleagues to call on for help, guidance and moral support. But of course you may be solo – a one-person operation – the only information professional in your organization. Or you may be 'embedded' within a project team, physically separated from other information professionals within the organization. You may also be facing the challenge of setting up your own enquiry service from scratch, or reviving one that has been allowed to wither following the departure of a former staff member. On top of that, it might be a brand-new job, with all your new users waiting for you to deliver. If this is your situation now, or if you're thinking of moving on from your present job to face that challenge in the future, then Chapter 7 is devoted to you.

To recap . . .

- ■ **Quality check your answer before you deliver it.**
- ■ **Plan your oral or written presentation carefully.**
- ■ **Make sure you observe copyright and licensing requirements.**
- ■ **Use completed enquiries to improve your success rate and develop your service.**

Setting up – how do you start?

Establishing your own enquiry service from scratch

> **In this chapter you'll find out how to:**
>
> - discover what your users need
> - identify and choose sources and services that will meet their needs
> - exploit the sources you invest in
> - raise the profile of your service through branding, promotion and customer care
> - get help and support when you need it.

It's your first day in the new job. You've beaten off stiff competition, convinced a tough interview panel that you're the best candidate for them, and you're thrilled at the confidence they've shown by appointing you.

Perhaps it's a complete change of career direction for you. Maybe you've left the technical back-up and colleagues' support of a large public, college or corporate library for the challenge of a tiny information unit in a company or not-for-profit organization. Maybe you have a staff member to manage for the first time. Or maybe you're solo – a one-person operation, responsible for everything from the service development, through the budgeting and IT troubleshooting, right down to making the tea. You may have inherited an existing service, which has become rundown because your predecessor left months ago. Or you might be the first information professional your organization has ever employed, and you have the task of providing an entirely new service from scratch. Or perhaps you're not sitting in your own room at all, but embedded within a specialist team, dedicated to meeting their information needs and expected to show total commitment to the project.

Whatever your new circumstances, you're now the organization's information expert, and your new employer is looking to you to deliver. How on earth do you start?

Finding out what your users need

Fortunately, you won't be starting from a position of total ignorance. You will have prepared thoroughly for your interview by looking at the organization's website, reading its promotional literature and its annual report. You'll know the names of the senior people – possibly met one or two of them on your interview panel. And you will by now be thoroughly well versed in what the organization does and what its goals are. All of this is vital data in your quest for ways of making yourself indispensable. When you finally arrive to start the job, what you need in addition is detailed intelligence on the information needs of the organization's key decision-makers. So your first priority should be to meet as many of them as possible at the earliest opportunity.

Meeting the top people

This may not be easy. Key decision-makers are by definition busy people, and they may not see the immediate benefit of setting aside time to be quizzed. They may even have fearsome PAs whose job is to protect them from approaches by people just like you. The important thing is not to let yourself be put off, although you may have to adopt a more subtle approach to secure the meetings you need.

However far down the hierarchy you feel yourself to be, there will be at least one or two more senior people to whom you do have an entrée: the ones who interviewed you. So approach them and ask them for introductions to their colleagues. If you do this, you'll probably get a sympathetic hearing – both from them and from the colleagues to whom they introduce you. Your interview panel members will already have had an opportunity to assess you and compare you with other candidates, and will know that you're not a time-waster. Their reputation will be on the line too, because they're the ones who have taken the decision to invest in you, and they will recognize that they must now help you to succeed. And the colleagues to whom they introduce you may well now be curious to meet this new addition to the organization, which comes with such a high recommendation.

Who to target

So you need to try to decide which of the organization's decision-makers are likely to be the most in need of information. This will enable you to draw up a list of your top targets and tick them off as you meet them.

This isn't an exact science, of course, but you may take the view that certain of the organization's functions are so routine that they are less likely to have unpredictable information needs that they can't satisfy from their own internal resources. You might, for example, put the Head of Finance or the Head of Personnel into this category, because they are largely providing routine support services – paying the bills, sending out the invoices, chasing the debts, paying the salaries, sorting out tax and insurance. However, you shouldn't rule them out entirely as potential clients. Finance may suddenly come to you for background information on a bad payer. Personnel may have an urgent need for a law report that establishes a precedent in a disciplinary case. But you can probably safely regard these kinds of enquiry as the exception rather than the rule.

Other senior colleagues are much more likely to have regular information needs that they can't easily satisfy for themselves. These may include the heads of:

- **Research**: looking for background information on the environment in which the organization is operating, or on social or economic issues that may affect it.
- **Business Development**: seeking information on new markets or activities into which the organization is considering expanding.
- **Competitive Intelligence**: watching out for threats against which the organization needs to protect itself, or opportunities to win business from competitors.
- **External Relations**: gathering background information on other bodies with which your organization works or is considering going into partnership.
- **Risk Management**: scanning the event horizon for any developments against which the organization may have to safeguard itself.

These are just a few examples – and, of course, the actual job titles will vary from one organization to another. So you will need to use your experience and, above all, your imagination to work out in advance which are your best targets and what their information needs are likely to be. In fact, you'll be doing exactly the same as you've always done when deciding how to tackle new enquiries – imagining what the final answer will look like.

The meeting

Once you've secured a date and time for your meeting, it's vital not to spoil the opportunity by going to it unprepared. Firstly, you need to know in advance how long it is scheduled to last. This may be your one and only opportunity in a long time to quiz the decision-maker concerned, so you must ensure that you are able to cover your entire agenda in the time available. Fortunately, your enquiry handling experience will help you here too. Remember Kipling's six honest serving men? You can use them to structure your precious meeting time with the decision-makers. Examples of questions you might consider asking include:

- **Who** are you? You'll know the name and job title of the person you're meeting, of course, but will need to find out about the department they head, including its structure and divisions.
- **What** does your department do? This is where you find out in more detail what falls within the department's specific remit, e.g. how do the functions of the Sales Department differ from those of Marketing, or how does the role of the External Relations Department overlap with that of the Overseas Department.
- **When** do you find that you need information you can't provide for yourself? Is there a pattern to the department's year – an especially urgent need for information towards the end of the financial year, or in the run up to the organization's annual general meeting, for example?
- **Where** do you get your information from at the moment? This is your opportunity to find out about the sources and delivery media the department currently uses. Bear in mind that it might not be using the best tools for the job. Or you may even discover that most of the information it uses is inside people's heads.
- **Why** do you need this information? This is your opportunity to discover more about what the department does, so you can understand the reasons behind its information needs.
- **How** do you manage the information you keep in the department? This can help you to start considering whether you can meet some of its

information needs more efficiently than it can, thereby reducing its costs and demonstrating your own value.

As is always the case when you're taking enquiries, you wouldn't necessarily ask the questions in this order, and certainly not in this form. The decision-maker will probably volunteer some of the answers – maybe even most of them – leaving you to ensure that all the ground has been covered and knowing exactly what final issues you still need to address as the meeting comes to a close. And, just as with your previous enquirers, you will encounter decision-makers who are generalists, know-alls, obsessively secretive – even muddlers. (Go back to Chapter 1 if you want a refresher in the various questioning strategies and techniques you can employ.)

Follow-up: managing initial expectations

You're almost inevitably going to come away from at least some of these meetings with an enquiry or two to tackle straight away. In fact, you may find that people are so delighted and relieved that there's an information professional finally in post that they offload months' if not years' worth of accumulated queries onto you, and of course expect an instant solution. Obviously you're going to have to manage their expectations if you're not to risk your own as yet untried reputation by promising too much too soon. Nevertheless you will have to provide something as early as possible, and all your previously acquired skills will come into play again. (Check back to Chapter 5 for ideas on how you might do this.)

First, you'll need to work out what is easy and quick to deliver, and what is hard and slow, and prioritize your responses on that basis. Remember, this is so that everyone gets something to read at the earliest possible opportunity. At first, quite a lot of what you're asked for is likely to be hard and slow, because you're still learning about your new organization and the information sources that serve it. So you'll probably need to provide lots of rough and ready answers in the first instance as an earnest of good faith, and to keep your enquirers informed about progress as you find out more on their behalf.

Second, you'll need to start working out whose needs are vital to the organization, and who is simply making use of you because you're there. When you're starting out on a new job, and eager to please whoever comes along, it's all too easy to become embroiled in the detailed requirements of people who are frankly more demanding than their importance merits.

There's no easy way of dealing with this once you've been sucked in, so the important thing is to be aware of the risk and learn to recognize it when it comes along. There are some danger signs you can spot: the enquirer who comes back day after day with one little query after another; the person who tries to butter you up by lavishing far more praise on you than you think your efforts merit; the type who claims that they have been personally asked to look into something by the chief executive or chairman, and implies that heads will roll if their requirements aren't given top priority.

Frequently, a discreet phone call to your favoured mentor within the organization (your line manager, perhaps, or your tame interview panel member) may be sufficient to establish how important the demanding enquirer's needs really are. This can enable you to assign a more appropriate degree of priority to their demands, in the reasonable certainty that you will be backed up if they complain.

Identifying the sources that will meet your users' needs

Dealing with these *ad hoc* enquiries, gathered as a result of your initial meetings, will kick-start your knowledge of the information sources and services that may be available to you – and the decision-makers you meet are almost bound to mention some of the key sources themselves. This will give you a useful shortlist to investigate, and two types are likely to predominate. Firstly, there will be tried and tested print publications that the department or its head have been using for years – industry directories, buyers' guides, trade magazines. Secondly, there will be websites – probably large numbers of them. Most people in the organization, if not all, are likely to have access to the internet on their desks, so it's pretty much inevitable that they will have used it to try to satisfy for themselves requests for information that will now become your responsibility.

It will certainly be worth following up any and all sources suggested by the people you have met. But don't fall into the trap of assuming that that's all you will need to do. It's very unlikely that any of these people will have taken an overview of all the potentially useful sources. It's far more likely that they will be using the sources they do because they are both available and familiar (irrespective of whether they are the best tools for the job). In fact, it's quite likely that they will have accumulated their clutch of favourite websites through little more than haphazard browsing, colleagues' recommendations and serendipity.

The questions you need to ask yourself first

Once you've met the key decision-makers you need to consider what you have learned about your organization and to start working out for yourself what sources will satisfy its needs. You may be starting from scratch, with nothing but your colleagues' unmet information needs to go on, or you may have inherited a room full of publications – books, reference materials, journals – from a long departed predecessor. You may also have encountered searching aids – catalogues, know-how files, resource lists, web links – that your predecessor maintained. Any or all of this may be helpful to you, but you should still go back to basics and ask yourself four fundamental questions:

1 What's going on in my organization's specialism now?
2 Who are the major players?
3 How are they communicating with each other?
4 How do I find out about earlier developments?

Finding out what's happening now

For finding out what's going on in your organization's specialism now, your best starting point is almost certainly the trade and professional media – whether delivered in print or electronically. You may well find print copies of some of the relevant titles in your organization already – either in your own information unit or lying around on colleagues' desks – and you should have discovered from some of the people you've met what trade and professional websites they regularly use. Then you'll need to check to make sure you haven't missed any other important trade or professional sources; the list of Starter Sources in Chapter 8 will help you discover what's available.

Having decided which sources you need to consider, you don't necessarily have to commit yourself to subscribing to them straight away. Your chosen titles will undoubtedly have websites, enabling you to see at least some representative content, on the basis of which you can start deciding whether or not to subscribe – or you can contact the publishers for a sample printed copy.

Trade and professional media are only the starting point for finding out what's happening now. In addition there will be discussion lists, blogs, news websites (maybe with feeds) that you will also need to consider. But trade and professional media provide an excellent key to unlock all these other resources. (We'll return to ways in which you can exploit them later.)

Identifying the major players

These sources will also start giving you clues as to who are the major players in your organization's specialism. They will be the organizations and individuals whose names keep coming up on the news pages, in feeds and in blogs. To make contact with them, and to find out more about what they do and how they're structured, you'll also need to know about the directories that are published in your specialism. As with the trade media, there are directories in every imaginable specialism, available in both print and electronic form. There are bound to be one or two that will prove useful to your organization. So again, take a look at the Starter Sources in Chapter 8 to help you identify suitable ones.

Directory publishers are less likely than the trade media to let you have sample printed copies on approval, but they will almost certainly have websites where you will be able to get a good feel for their publications' content and coverage. You may even be able to interrogate some of them online, on a pay-as-you-go basis, before deciding whether or not to subscribe.

The other type of major player to consider in your field is the range of professional and trade bodies that regulate your organization's specialism and act as a forum for its members. Plenty of directories (see the Starter Sources) will give you brief details of the bodies you need to be aware of. Crucially, these directories will give you their web addresses; professionally edited and quality controlled, directories are a much more reliable way of finding the bodies you need on the web than simply using a search engine.

Discovering how these players are communicating with one another

Even though they may be in competition – for customers if they are profit-seeking organizations, for members or funding if not-for-profit – the players in your organization's specialist field will also be communicating with each other in a myriad different ways. Their representatives will be attending conferences and giving papers, debating current topics on discussion lists, writing to the trade and professional media, entering into partnerships or consortia, jointly publishing reports. It's going to be a challenge for you to keep up with this huge volume of activity; you'll almost certainly have to be selective in what you monitor.

If you do have to pick just one way of monitoring all this communication then, again, basic trade media are probably the best single source. It's the job of trade journalists not only to know what's going on but also to know what's important for your specialism – and at the same time, press offices and public relations firms representing all the players in the field will be feeding those journalists with news items. Many of the news stories and articles that the trade media cover will refer to newly published reports or conference papers – and they'll frequently include a web address where you can download those reports or their executive summaries.

You can wait for the next printed issue of your chosen trade journal or journals to come out if you wish. Or increasingly you can take a feed, with news items delivered to you online as they break – frequently in advance of their publication in the printed journal. (We'll return to the question of exploiting your information sources shortly.)

Finding out about earlier developments

The sources and strategies we've considered already will help you keep up with what's going on now. But you will need to consider yet further sources for searching the archives of your specialism's accumulated knowledge down the years. As with the trade media and the directories, there are innumerable searchable archives of professional and academic journals, conference papers and reports. Some are owned by large scale academic and professional journal publishers, and feature only titles from their own publishing stable. Others are created by specialist bodies in the field – research institutes, professional associations, academic faculties or consortia, commercial publishers. You'll need to find out which ones you should consider providing to your users (see Chapter 8).

Customer needs first – sources second

With all the demands for information that you are likely to be faced with from day one, it would be tempting to start acquiring sources straight away. Resist the temptation if you can. You really do need to be sure that you're buying the most cost-effective sources and services for your organization, in the most appropriate delivery media. So do try to have those meetings with key decision-makers first. As soon as they know you're in the market – because you've asked for a sample copy of a trade magazine, for example, or registered to use a website – publishers will start bombarding you with flyers and e-mails containing tempting offers. By the time that starts happening, you need to be sure that you really do know what you need, so you're not swayed by publishers' blandishments.

All the same, you shouldn't dismiss all this promotional material as junk mail. It's actually likely to be pretty well targeted to your requirements, and you can expect it to become even more so as you keep returning to useful websites and they start serving up targeted ads. So give each communication just a few seconds' consideration before you drop it in the waste-paper basket or hit the delete key; every so often, your hand will be stayed because you've spotted something potentially useful. The important thing to remember, though, is that your stock and selection policies should be driven by your organization's needs – and you have to know what those needs are first.

Exploiting your sources

Once you've invested in all those sources, should you just let them lie fallow and wait for people to come along and discover them? Absolutely not! Once the initial flurry of interest in your arrival has died down, you'll need to constantly refresh your users' interest. Without too much difficulty, you can use your newly acquired sources both to promote your information service and to add to its resources.

Trade media

Once again, there's no better place to start than the trade media in all their delivery forms – printed magazine, website, feed, blog (and microblog), discussion list, searchable archive.

Let's start with the printed publication. If it's typical of the usual format, it will have news stories (probably written by staff journalists), feature articles (some by journalists, some by guest writers), regular opinion pieces (probably by specialists in the subject who have a flair for writing as well), book and product reviews (contributed by specialists as a rule), possibly an irreverent end piece, and masses of ads, both display and classified. You can make use of all of these.

Take a look at the **news stories**. See how many of them are based on other literature – newly published reports or surveys, for example. The news story will usually tell you where you can get hold of the report. You might then decide to buy it in print, or provide a link to the electronic version on your intranet, or download a PDF and store it locally where anyone in your organization can read it. Beware – you need to ensure that you are operating within copyright law and observing the publisher's licensing conditions if you do this. But whatever you decide to do, you've added both to your resources and to the value of your service.

A glance at the **articles and opinion pieces** will tell you what the hot issues are at the moment, and who's talking about them. So when a senior manager or – worse – their dragon of a PA phones up and barks a request for information on a new topic, you should at least recognize the buzzwords used and recall that you have seen something about it. That should be sufficient to enable you to go back to the publication's website and seek out the article in its charged-for, password-protected area.

The **reviews** can help you identify core literature – new editions of standard textbooks, for example – that you may need to acquire to bolster your collection. The **display ads** are your guide to sources and services that support your organization's specialism and the **classifieds** are your up-to-date buyer's guide.

So do get into the habit of giving every issue of each printed title a few minutes' attention when it comes in. Just ten minutes skimming through can be a really worthwhile investment of your time.

Professional and academic journals

These are a different kind of beast from the trade media. Sober and restrained in appearance, they're likely to contain a comparatively small number of lengthy articles, written by specialists in the field and including plenty of supporting detail and references to further literature. Many of the articles may be worth recording in your own retrieval system as separate information sources in their own right. And the lists of references included with particularly pertinent articles may lead you to publications that you need to acquire to further enhance your core collection.

Another good way of exploiting professional and academic journals is to alert your organization to their contents. You can do this quite simply – by creating a classified list of the articles in a newly received journal and e-mailing it round the organization or to selected users, or posting the information on your intranet or in-house social network. Sometimes you'll find the journal publisher – who will probably try hard to keep you locked into their products – will help you with this, giving you access to special alerting applications that you can use to direct the right content to the right user.

Feeds, blogs, microblogs, discussion lists

Valuable as all these conventionally published sources are, they're only the beginning. Feeds, blogs, microblogs and discussion lists can all add to your information resources and raise the profile of your service. What do they do, how can you identify them and how can you decide what to use?

Feeds provide an easy way for you to automatically keep up to date on the websites you want to track regularly. Instead of having to visit sites to see if they've changed, you can use a feed to be told whenever they add something new. Quite a few web browsers can support feeds directly – but if yours doesn't, you'll need to use feed aggregator (or feed reader or news reader) software, either on the web or installed locally on your machine or network. Of course, you don't necessarily need to take all these feeds yourself; you could simply advise colleagues that feeds of especial interest to them are available, and if necessary help them set up a feed for themselves.

Blogs have already come up in Chapter 4. There are millions of them and their numbers are growing fast, so you will need to be very selective in the ones you choose to follow. So why not start again with your trusty trade and professional media? Expert columnists who write regularly for these publications may well have their own blogs, which they will very likely promote in their columns, so this could be a useful way of identifying blogs that will genuinely have something valuable to say. Blogs frequently incorporate feeds as well, so you don't even need to visit them regularly in order to keep up with them. As with feeds, the danger with blogs is that you will be tempted to take so much information by this medium that you rapidly have more than you can cope with. So, instead of taking them for yourself, you could simply keep track of what's available, provide links to them on your intranet, and alert your users to specific blogs that you think they might be interested in taking for themselves.

Microblogs are even more likely to overwhelm you with more material than you can handle, if you let them. Limited for technical reasons to 140 characters, they're an ideal medium for the off-the-cuff (and sometimes ill-considered) comment. But again, if you decide to follow a corporate microblog, or one compiled by an expert in the field, this can be an invaluable source of up to the minute alerts. And microblogs can also include specially shortened web addresses leading you to more detailed content.

Discussion lists are online forums to which a community of people contributes. The messages from each contributor are frequently organized as navigable discussion 'threads' on particular topics, accessible via a website.

Individual contributions (or postings) are also delivered to all the list members by e-mail, either as soon as they are posted or else in batches at regular intervals. Discussion lists may be closed – accessible by a particular group of people only – or open – available to anyone who wants to register to use them. Some discussion lists are moderated, which means that there is someone with an editorial role ensuring, for example, that lists don't get overloaded with trivia or repetition, and that contributors treat each other courteously. Others are not, and can become so anarchic and acrimonious as to be well nigh useless as a serious information source. Again, you may want to keep yourself aware of relevant discussion lists, and post links to them on your intranet so that your users can join them if they wish.

And lastly – your own organization's expertise

One crucial source that you really can't afford to ignore is the expertise locked up in the heads of people in your organization and the internal documents they produce. So is there a list anywhere giving people's expertise? Is there a corporate know-how resource to which specialists in the organization contribute? Is there a policy for managing unstructured documents – the wealth of potential knowledge that's sitting in e-mails, memos, minutes, presentations, discussion threads? And if no resources like this exist currently, should it be part of your job to set them up?

Promoting your service

Whatever kind of information service you provide, you can't afford to simply sit back and wait for people to come. This matters if your organization operates out of one site and all your users are in the same building – but it matters even more if they are scattered throughout the country or even the world. We've already seen how you need to start by getting to know your users and their needs, and to segment them to ensure that the right services go to the right people. To protect your service, and ensure that it has the resources to develop when opportunity arises, you must also keep your profile high.

So consider inventing a special name for your service. Develop a corporate identity for it, based on your organization's logo, and add a strapline drawing attention to the value you can add. Keep your service in the public eye by regularly telling your users what's new – and concentrate on the benefits that you can deliver, not on the sources you have acquired. Encourage your best initial users to become advocates and champions for your service, recommending it to other decision-makers who might not have been prepared to see you the first time. And when pitching to any potential new user, concentrate on their needs, not on your sources.

You also need to lock your users in by constantly feeding them fresh information – through a current awareness or selective dissemination of information (SDI) service for example, based on material you find in the trade or professional media. Your users will probably be able to access many of the new sources you highlight directly over the web; so regard this as an opportunity to free your time up for fresh developments rather than a threat to you as the organization's information gateway. If you help your users to become self-sufficient in answering their own routine enquiries, and concentrate on the difficult ones yourself, that can only enhance your reputation, not diminish it.

E-mail may seem the obvious main medium for communicating your message – but some people are now starting to question its effectiveness in an organization and its impact on corporate time management. Increasingly, too, new and younger recruits will be accustomed to communicating via social media rather than e-mail. So make good use of whatever social and collaborative tools your organization offers – whether these be access to publicly available social networks and microblogging services or specially installed proprietary software to manage information sharing and project collaboration.

Getting help and support

Running a small information unit can be a lonely and isolating experience – especially if you're the only information professional in the organization. You'll need help and support – practical and moral – from time to time. And you'll certainly need advice on how you can do your job better. Fortunately this is a very supportive profession, and there's no shortage of places you can turn to for help. To follow up any of the ideas in the sections below, and find organizations and networks that may be able to help you, check out the Starter Sources in Chapter 8 – particularly the section on finding contacts for further information. Following are some sources of help and support that you could look for.

Fellow information workers

Although you may feel isolated, you certainly won't be alone. There will be fellow information professionals working in similar organizations to yours, whose brains you can pick for ideas to develop your service further. You may be able to identify some of them through the directories relating to your organization's specialism that you will have acquired by now. Alternatively, there are plenty of other directories available that can help you find sources of help and support.

This won't be a one-way process, of course; you must expect to have your brains picked in return. You'll also need to bear in mind that your supportive fellow information professional may be working for one of your competitors. However, this shouldn't prevent you from making contact; you both just need to ensure that you restrict your discussions to matters of professional practice, and don't risk giving away confidential information.

Professional associations

You can get plenty of further support from your professional peers by joining some of the multiplicity of membership organizations and special interest groups that the library and information profession spawns. First of all, they'll provide a range of publications that will enable you to keep up to date with developments. In addition, going to meetings of professional groups may prove less hazardous than meeting follow professionals informally on a one-to-one basis; group meetings are more likely to be held on neutral territory, so there's less likelihood of participants laying themselves open to possible accusations of collusion with competitors. Bigger associations usually have their own special interest groups, and there are also smaller but no less lively independent associations and networks, which may mainly operate virtually but also hold regular meetings in hired premises.

Online discussion lists

If you can't easily get to meetings, then you may well be able to participate virtually by joining an online discussion list. Once again, their numbers are legion and there can be few professional groups in the information field that don't offer some kind of online discussion facility. Just like the people who contribute to them, discussion lists tend to have good days and bad days. Sometimes you'll encounter really useful discussions about information sources that can help with a particularly difficult enquiry. At other times the same discussion lists seem to be offering nothing but gripes.

Training and guides

As you develop your enquiry service, there will be plenty of other things you'll need to know that are outside the scope of this book. You may need to learn the basics of cataloguing and classification (or metadata and taxonomies if you prefer), so you can manage your collection efficiently and make it accessible to your users. You may decide to use a database package for this purpose and be looking for a refresher in using that effectively too. You'll need to find out about interlibrary loan and document delivery services, and about copyright and licensing, to ensure that the copying and downloading you do doesn't infringe intellectual property rights. You'll want to buy equipment and software – something as basic as shelving and furniture, or as sophisticated as a radio-frequency identification (RFID) self-issuing system or a networked enquiry management package. For all of these needs and more, help is at hand in the form of training and practical guides.

Several library and information organizations (and some of their special interest groups), plus a number of independent trainers, offer courses in every aspect of running an information service, and specialist publishers put out scores of practical handbooks (just like this one), covering other topics that we haven't been able to touch on here. And when it comes to sourcing equipment and services, ads in library and information journals and websites – plus the odd buyer's guide – can help you find what you need.

Coming last – choosing your toolkit...

We're almost there, but there's still one thing left to do – choose the actual resources that you're going to need to enable you to run your enquiry service effectively. We've scarcely mentioned any products or publications by name so far, but have focused instead on the techniques you need to employ to ensure your service runs smoothly. But now's the time to bite the bullet and invest in some specific tools. So in Chapter 8, we'll look at some of the resources you might consider.

To recap . . .

■ **Start by finding out what your users need – then make sure that your information resources will meet those needs.**

■ **Use your sources to find out what's going on in your organization's specialism now, who the major players are, and how they are communicating with each other.**

■ **Exploit your information sources to raise the profile of your service.**

■ **Don't be afraid to look for professional help and support.**

CHAPTER 8

Choosing your toolkit

Resources that you'll need to run your enquiry service

In this chapter you'll find links to:

- **search engines**
- **enquiry tracking software**
- **Starter Sources.**

Up to now we've tended not to mention specific sources or products by name but just to refer to them generically. This is a manual about skills, after all – not a directory. But if you've stuck with us this far, you'll be aware that we've referred to search engines, enquiry management systems – and above all specific information sources that can get you started on a whole range of enquiries. So here's a selection of resources that you might find useful in your enquiry work. None of the lists in this chapter are exhaustive, and professional peers may dispute some of the choices. But hopefully they'll be enough to give you a flying start.

Search engines

There is actually more than one! In fact there are hundreds. So here are a couple of places where you can check out others and see how they vary from one another:

Which Search Engine When? (Phil Bradley)
    www.philb.com/whichengine.htm
Search Tools Summary and Comparison (RBA Information Services)
    HTML version: www.rba.co.uk/search/compare.shtml
    PDF version: www.rba.co.uk/search/compare.pdf

Enquiry tracking software

We've made clear throughout the book that you can operate a much more efficient enquiry service if you use some kind of software package to help you manage your work. Automating your enquiry management will provide useful performance data as well. So here are some software packages and services that are suitable for keeping track of enquiries. Some are specifically designed for library and information enquiry management, but some need to be adapted from other applications. Their functionality, availability and delivery media vary too – so check them out individually if you want to follow any of them up.

Specifically designed for library and information enquiries

Eos.Web Enterprise Reference Tracking (Eos International)
　　www.eosintl.com/Products/Enterprise/Enterprise_RefTrack.aspx
KnowAll Enquiry Tracking (Bailey Solutions)
　　www.baileysolutions.co.uk/enquiry-tracking
QuestionPoint (OCLC)
　　www.oclc.org/questionpoint/default.htm
RefTracker (Altarama)
　　www.altarama.com.au/reftrack.htm
Text a Librarian (Mosio)
　　www.textalibrarian.com

Designed for other applications (frequently IT helpdesks) but can be adapted

BMC Remedy (BMC)
　　www.bmc.com/products/product-listing/22735072-106757-2391.html
Footprints (Numara)
　　www.numarasoftware.com/footprints.asp
Lagan (Lagan)
　　http://www.kana.com/lagan/online-government-software/stack.php
OpenScape (Siemens Enterprise Communications)
　　www.siemens-enterprise.com/uk/products/contact-center-solutions.aspx
RightNow Contact Center Experience (RightNow Technologies)
　　www.rightnow.com/cx-suite-contact-center-experience.php

Supportworks (Hornbill)
   www.hornbill.com/products/esp

And not forgetting these Microsoft products, which can also be adapted for the purpose...

Access
   http://office.microsoft.com/en-gb/access/FX100487571033.aspx
Excel
   http://office.microsoft.com/en-gb/excel/FX100487621033.aspx
Sharepoint
   www.microsoftbusinesshub.com/Products/Microsoft_Sharepoint

Starter Sources

Finally, some professionally edited information sources that can get you started on an incredibly wide range of enquiries. One or more of them will frequently be your first port of call once you've imagined what the final answer will look like. Most of them are charged for, although a few are free. Many are available in more than one medium – print, online, mobile, portable. Some are print only. They'll not only provide quality-checked information that you can rely on – they can frequently also direct you to reliable websites. Some sources have more than one use – so they'll crop up more than once in the Starter Sources list. Where a service is charged, the link shown here will usually take you to a description of it; if the service is free, the link will usually allow you to use it straight away.

The notes about their geographic coverage require a little clarification. The sources that claim world coverage frequently offer only patchy information about developing nations. 'American' coverage may mean just the United States or could include other North American countries. 'Europe' could refer to the whole continent, or the European Economic Area, or just the European Union. And coverage of 'Britain' sometimes also takes in Ireland or can be restricted to the British mainland.

Identifying basic reference sources
World

New Walford Guide to Reference Sources

1: Science, Technology, Medicine
2: Social Sciences
3: Arts
www.facetpublishing.co.uk (Then follow links. Publication is print only.)
UlrichsWeb Global Serials Directory
http://ulrichsweb.serialssolutions.com

Britain/World

Know It All, Find It Fast
Know It All, Find It Fast for Academic Libraries
Know It All, Find It Fast for Youth Librarians and Teachers
www.facetpublishing.co.uk (Then follow links. Publications are print only.)

Identifying and tracing books
World

British Library Integrated Catalogue
    http://catalogue.bl.uk
Bowker's Global Books in Print
    www.globalbooksinprint.com
Nielsen BookData
    www.nielsenbookdata.co.uk

America/Europe/Britain

Google Books
    http://books.google.com

Britain

British National Bibliography
    www.bl.uk/bibliographic/natbib.html

Tracing items to consult, borrow or buy
World

WorldCat

www.worldcat.org (Items to consult or borrow)
Google Scholar
   http://scholar.google.com (Items to consult)
Amazon
   www.amazon.com (Items to buy)

Identifying journals and newspapers
World

Ulrichsweb Global Serials Directory
   http://ulrichsweb.serialssolutions.com
Willing's Press Guide
   http://uk.cision.com/Products-and-Services/media-database/
   print-directories/Willings

Tracing and acquiring articles
World

British Library Direct
   http://direct.bl.uk
British Library Inside
   www.bl.uk/reshelp/atyourdesk/docsupply/productsservices/inside
JSTOR
   www.jstor.org

America/World

HW Wilson Databases
   www.ebscohost.com/wilson

Britain/World

Abstracts in New Technologies and Engineering
   www.csa.com/factsheets/ante-set-c.php
Applied Social Sciences Index and Abstracts
   www.csa.com/factsheets/assia-set-c.php
British Humanities Index
   www.csa.com/factsheets/bhi-set-c.php

Sociological Abstracts
www.csa.com/factsheets/socioabs-set-c.php

Single publisher's output

EBSCO
www.ebsco.com
Emerald Insight
www.emeraldinsight.com
ingentaconnect
www.ingentaconnect.com
Sage Journals
http://online.sagepub.com

Finding reliable material on unanticipated subjects
World

Google Scholar
http://scholar.google.com
ProQuest Dialog
www.dialog.com
LexisNexis
www.lexisnexis.com

Britain

CORE: COnnecting REpositories
http://core.kmi.open.ac.uk/search

Finding facts and figures
World

Europa World Plus
www.europaworld.com/pub
Central Intelligence Agency (CIA): The World Factbook
www.cia.gov/cia/publications/factbook/index.html
Statesman's Yearbook
www.statesmansyearbook.com

Britain/World

Whitaker's Almanac
   www.whitakersalmanack.co.uk

Tracing events, dates and news items
World

Google News
   http://news.google.com
Keesing's World News Archive
   www.keesings.com
Plus, of course, thousands of news media, press agency, broadcast organization and expert blogger websites.

Identifying and tracing statistics
World

Offstats: Official Statistics on the Web
   www.offstats.auckland.ac.nz
United Nations Statistics Division
   http://unstats.un.org/unsd

World/Europe

European Marketing Data & Statistics
International Marketing Data & Statistics
World Economic Factbook
   www.euromonitor.com/books (Then follow links.)

Europe

Eurostat
   http://ec.europa.eu/eurostat

Britain

UK National Statistics
   www.statistics.gov.uk

Sources of Non-Official UK Statistics
www.gowerpub.com/default.aspx?page=637&calcTitle=1&title_id=
8749&edition_id=9336

Finding contacts for further information
World

Associations Unlimited
www.gale.cengage.com/servlet/ItemDetailServlet?region=9&imprint=
000&titleCode=GAL7&type=4&id=110996
The Europa World of Learning
www.worldoflearning.com
Hollis PR
www.hollis-pr.com
World Guide to Libraries
www.degruyter.de (Then follow links.)
Yearbook of International Organizations
www.uia.be/yearbook

Britain

Councils, Committees & Boards
Centres, Bureaux & Research Institutes
Directory of British Associations and Associations in Ireland
www.cbdresearch.com

Final word of warning

Information on sources and delivery media can go out of date incredibly
quickly. As far as possible, we confirmed that all the information in this
chapter was up to date at the time the book was published, but there may well
have been changes since. If you can't trace a source listed in this chapter and
would like to see if more up to date information is available, or if you discover
that a link no longer works, contact Facet Publishing and ask to be put in
touch with the author, Tim Buckley Owen.

Your goal: successful enquiry answering – every time

So that's it! With a little care and common sense – plus a lively and imaginative approach – you can make enquiry answering one of the most satisfying and fulfilling work activities there is. The explosion of available information, the technological developments that can help you retrieve and enhance it, and the enormously increased awareness of the value of information – all combine to make the prospects for library and information professionals more exciting than ever before. All you need to do is to grasp those opportunities. So the only thing that remains is to wish you success with your enquiry answering – every time.

To recap . . .

- **There is more than one search engine – check out the benefits and limitations of others.**
- **Plenty of software packages can help you manage your enquiries better.**
- **Just a limited number of sources can get you started on a wide range of enquiries.**

Index